D0734583

OUT OF THE BLUE
YOUNG READER'S EDITION

VICTOR CRUZ

WITH PETER SCHRAGER

A CELEBRA CHILDREN'S BOOK

OUT OF THE BLUE

YOUNG READER'S EDITION

Celebra Children's Books
Published by New American Library, a division of
Penguin Group (USA) Inc., 375 Hudson Street, New York, New York 10014, USA

USA/Canada/UK/Ireland/Australia/New Zealand/India/South Africa/China
Penguin Books Ltd, Registered Offices: 80 Strand, London WC2R 0RL, England

For more information about the Penguin Group visit penguin.com

Young Reader's edition first published by Celebra Children's Books
a division of Penguin Group (USA) Inc.

Library of Congress Cataloging-in-Publication Data
Cruz, Victor, date.
Out of the blue / by Victor Cruz with Peter Schrager. — Young reader's edition.
pages   cm
ISBN 978-0-451-41997-2 (hardcover)
1. Cruz, Victor, date. 2. Football players—United States—Biography.
3 Wide receivers (Football)—United States—Biography. I. Title.
GV939.C783A3 2013
796.332092—dc23
[B]
2012050368

Printed in the United States of America

10 9 8 7 6 5 4 3 2 1

Book design by Jasmin Rubero
Text set in Aptifer Slab LT Pro

CELEBRA and logo are trademarks of Penguin Group (USA) Inc.

PUBLISHER'S NOTE

Penguin is committed to publishing works of quality and integrity. In that
spirit, we are proud to offer this book to our readers; however, the story, the
experiences and the words are the author's alone.
    While the author has made every effort to provide accurate telephone
numbers, Internet addresses, and other contact information at the time of
publication, neither the publisher nor the author assumes any responsibility
for errors, or for changes that occur after publication. Further, publisher does
not have any control over and does not assume any responsibility for author
or third-party Web sites or their content.

This book is dedicated to my dad, Michael Walker, and my grandfather Fernando DeJesus. May you rest in peace and watch over my family and me.

CONTENTS

OUT OF THE BLUE
PROLOGUE

THIRD AND TEN.

Two minutes, twenty-seven seconds left in the first half.

The ball was on our own one yard line. We were down 7–3 to the Jets.

Antonio Cromartie, the Jets cornerback, was staring me right in the eye. Cromartie's a talker. He told me I was a "no name." He said that I didn't belong on the field.

Cromartie had every right to be jawing.

So far I'd done nothing the whole game. Earlier in the week, Mario Manningham and I had said a few things about Cro's Jets teammate Darrelle Revis. The quotes had ended up on the back pages of the city's major newspapers. One headline read CRUZ SAYS TEAMS AREN'T SCARED OF REVIS ANYMORE.

That wasn't *quite* what I had said, but that's what was printed and pasted up on the Jets' bulletin board. Welcome to New York.

But it was Cromartie who had answered back, not Revis. When a reporter had asked him about Mario's comments, he said, "We'll have to see on Saturday. That's even if he touches the field. He let a guy named Victor Cruz come in and take his job."

A guy named Victor Cruz.

Like it was some shameful thing.

It was Christmas Eve. We were playing the Jets at MetLife Stadium. In East Rutherford, New Jersey. It's our home building, but it's the Jets' home building too. On the NFL schedule this was a Jets home game. At every other game we'd played at MetLife, we had lined up on the sideline to the east of the field. For this one, we were the "visiting" team. So we were standing on the west sideline. You wouldn't think that would matter, but it was throwing us off.

Before kickoff, I scanned the stands—our stands—and it was just a sea of Jets green. That Fireman Ed dude was on his buddy's shoulders leading the *"J-e-t-s, Jets, Jets, Jets!"* chant.

There was a bloodlust in the air.

It had been an ugly, sloppy game. Our defense had bailed us out all afternoon, and we were lucky to be down just four points.

THIRTEEN YEARS EARLIER, about fifteen miles to the north, I was wearing double pads and a red, white, and blue mesh jersey for my Little League football team, the PAL North Firefighters.

My father was a firefighter in Paterson, New Jersey. All the other kids on the team were either sons or nephews of Paterson firefighters too. I played center on that squad. I hiked the ball to the quarterback. I blocked opposing blitzers.

I really liked playing center. I was a part of the action. Running play, passing play—I was always involved.

It was cool.

I was twelve years old, and I had this weird, little-kid body with really long arms and crazy long legs. I had a big neck too, like a giraffe. I wore thickly framed glasses and there was no meat on my bones.

I was happy playing center. But my dad, an assistant coach on the squad, would constantly be in the ear of our head coach, Mr. Tolbert.

"Give Victor a shot at tailback," my father would tell him. "Let Victor run the ball."

One game pretty late in the season, we were up by a few touchdowns. My father had spent much of the second half pestering Mr. Tolbert. Finally, I got called off the field.

"Victor, we're putting you in at fullback," he told me. "We're up by a lot of points. If you lose a few yards, that's okay. Just don't fumble the ball."

I lined up in the backfield for the first time of my life. Over on our sideline I spotted my father. His eyes were lit up. He was beaming.

It was as if he knew something I didn't.

"Hut one, hut two, hike . . ."

Nigel, our quarterback, handed me the ball and I remember just thinking, Don't fumble it. I shook one defender behind the line of scrimmage. Then I saw an opening over the right guard. Daylight. I shimmied left and shifted right, just like one of my idols, Emmitt Smith. I shed another tackle. I was past the line and in open space. I had just one man left to beat—a cornerback a foot shorter than me.

In a flash, I had to decide whether to barrel over this kid or just burn him on the outside. I went with option one.

Then I was gone. Sixty-four yards. Touchdown.

My father had sprinted down the sideline, running stride for stride with me, for the entire run. He was in the end zone, right there next to me, jumping up and down.

I gave him a big hug. On our way back to the sideline, my father skipped over to Coach Tolbert. "I told you so!" he shouted. "I told you so!"

I'd never play center another down in my life.

WE WERE 7-7 going into the Christmas Eve game. The Jets were 8-6. This was a must-win game for both teams if either wanted to make the playoffs.

As Cromartie and I stared at each other, I remembered the down and distance.

Third and ten.

The play called in from the sideline was a double hook route for Hakeem Nicks and me. A third receiver, Ramses Barden, was also lined up outside me. Both Hakeem and I were supposed to fight off coverage at the line of scrimmage, run about ten yards, and pivot to the out-side—Hakeem going left, me going right.

The play was designed so that as we both turned and pivoted, Ramses was supposed to fly past me down the sidelines, crossing toward the middle of the field.

Eli Manning settled into the shotgun, and our center, David Baas, snapped the ball. Eli stepped back and looked left to Hakeem, but Revis was draped all over him.

Just as I shifted right and began to pivot, Eli and I linked eyes.

The two of us had spent hours practicing this very route the previous summer. Running a hook route is very difficult on the body. You've got to make a hard plant with one leg, and then your entire body has to shift, turn, and smoothly dart the other way.

As I broke right, Eli unleashed a perfectly thrown ten-yard pass to my outside. I felt Kyle Wilson's right hand on the back of my jersey. He lunged at the ball, hoping to knock it down. I felt him overpursuing, pushed him off me, and caught the ball cleanly.

Cromartie was next. He had left Ramses and was coming at me head-on. In that instant, I thought about my touchdown runs for the PAL North Firefighters. I thought about my AAU basketball team, the Tim Thomas Playaz, and breaking free for a layup. I thought about the game in high school when I scored five touchdowns in the first half versus Elmwood Park.

As Cro came at me, I sidestepped him, pivoting hard to the inside. He lunged, but he was already on his knees. Too late, Cro.

I was gone.

Down the twenty. Down the thirty. Only one man to beat—Eric Smith. At the forty-five yard line, I looked into Smith's eyes. Defenders always have a look in their eyes. Sometimes it's hunger. Other times it's desperation. We both knew he had only one option—to dive at my legs.

Smith dove like Superman, his arms outstretched.

I did a little skip move. A hop step, really.

All Smith got was an armful of air.

Daylight.

I was the teenage kid running home from Montgomery Park after hearing gunshots. I was the guy practicing curl routes on an empty football field up in Bridgton, Maine. I was the dude doing a forty-yard dash on a college Pro Day.

I was a blur down the sideline. The fifty. The forty. The thirty.

At around the twenty yard line, I looked up above the end zone and into the crowd. I saw my mother and my girlfriend, Elaina, eight months pregnant at the time, going wild in that sea of green.

The ten.

Touchdown.

For the first time all afternoon, MetLife Stadium was silent. Nothing.

Then I heard boos. The Jets fans were booing me.

But then I realized, those weren't boos at all. They were saying, "Cruuuuuz."

They were saying *my* name.

Not bad for a guy named Victor Cruz.

HOMEGROWN

AS A KID, I saw the New York City skyline every single day of my life. The Big Apple was just a ten-minute ride away from my childhood home in Paterson, New Jersey. It was an easy commute.

But New York City might as well have been the Land of Oz, some magical world with streets paved of gold. In the first fifteen years of my life, I probably went to New York only three times.

New York City represented money, fame, and fortune. In Paterson, we had Italian combo heroes at Skuffy's Subs. We had the guy with the neon green nylon pants who was always posting up outside the bodega on Crooks Avenue. We had the barely paved parking lot with no backboards or rims that we turned into our own imaginary Madison Square Garden.

We had each other.

I GREW UP in my grandparents' home at 44 East Twentieth Street. It was a three-bedroom apartment on the third floor of a redbrick building. I had my own room, my mother had hers, and my *abuela,* my grandmother, and her husband had one too. On the first floor of the building was a Spanish bodega, El Aguila Supermarket. A man named Teddy was the owner and one of the great characters of my childhood. Any time I'd pop in for a juice box or a pack of basketball cards, Teddy would have a knock-knock joke or a noogie to give me in return.

My grandmother arrived in Paterson from Puerto Rico in 1965. She had no job, no home, no money, and my nine-year-old mother in tow. Life was hard. My grandmother's English wasn't very good, and she was a single mother. She eventually found work at a sewing factory, met my grandfather, and settled into that home on East Twentieth. My *abuela* was my everything, but my grandfather—my mother's stepfather—was my best friend. His full name was Fernando DeJesus, but he was always *Papí* to me.

Papí retired from his job of twenty years as a factory worker right before I was born in 1986. He was always shirtless in my memories of him. He'd wear the nicest, crispest brown slacks, a leather belt, beautiful polished shoes, and fancy argyle socks—but never a shirt. He was missing a finger from a factory accident he suffered in his twenties and had a huge scar down his back. My mother later told me that the scar was left after he had one of his lungs removed, the result of smoking too many cigarettes as a young man.

Every morning, *Papí* would wake up at exactly six thirty. He'd go to the breakfast table, and my grandmother would serve him his coffee—always black, no cream or sugar—in the same white mug. He'd then head over to his rocking chair, lay out his newspaper, and put on an old vinyl record.

That music, if I hear it now, still gives me goose bumps. It wasn't the salsa or anything upbeat. It was a man serenading a woman. The singer's name was José Feliciano, and his voice was like silk. It was beautiful. My grandfather would rock on that chair of his, put me on his lap, and just sing the same ten or eleven tunes in Spanish. I remember him telling me to listen not so much to the singer's words, but to the *way* he sang them. José Feliciano never rushed, he never screamed—he was always even keeled and well paced. "He lets the music breathe," my grandfather would say, "and that's how one should live his life."

We'd then hit Eastside Park and do laps around the greens all morning. I'd climb the trees, run on the fields, and play in the dirt. He'd be with me,

"HE LETS THE MUSIC BREATHE," MY GRANDFATHER WOULD SAY, "AND THAT'S HOW ONE SHOULD LIVE HIS LIFE."

13

always one step behind, humming his songs in Spanish and watching me explore.

My grandfather had his life in order. He always told me, "If your life is stable, the rest will fall into place." He ate three meals a day at the same exact time. At five o'clock every night, it was dinnertime. No matter what was going on in the park or on the street, whether it was "game point" in a basketball game or the bottom of the ninth in a stickball battle, I had to be at that dinner table at five p.m. No ifs, ands, or buts.

My grandmother knew that if I was in the house by five, at that dinner table, I couldn't be somewhere else getting into trouble. If I didn't make it back for dinner by five p.m., I wasn't eating that night. Plain and simple. And I liked to eat. My *abuela*'s food was incredible. You'd smell her pork chops cooking from a block away, and the thought of her arepas still makes my mouth water.

I'd play sports with all the other kids in the neighborhood on the street right beneath our apartment. At four fifty-five every day, she would scream from three stories up, "Victorrrrrr!" All the other kids would make fun of me, yelling "Victorrrrrr!" in their best sixty-year-old Puerto Rican woman voices.

One time, I ignored her screams for dinner. After a few minutes, my friend Corey said, "Um . . . Victor, I think your grandmother's coming." And when I turned around—there she was, storming down the street in her floral nightgown with my grandfather's black leather belt in her hand. She had curlers in her hair and fuzzy white slippers on, with the crazed look of a woman scorned.

The other kids were all dying of laughter. She came after me like Ray Lewis. I managed a shake and bake and darted up the stairs to the dinner table. Those moves you see on the football field on Sundays? Those weren't perfected at some fancy football summer camp. They were honed avoiding my grandmother's swinging belt on East Twentieth Street.

Papí and I always had fun even inside the house. I was a World Wrestling Federation freak. And guess what? So was he! My grandfather—who must have been in his early sixties—was obsessed with professional wrestling. Of all the amazing WWF characters, he loved the Undertaker the most. The Undertaker was this towering, pale, half-dead character who was supposed to be from the underworld. He had this really slow gait and radiated doom and dread. *Papí* would pretend that he was the Undertaker and chase me around the house. When I say "chase," I mean he'd walk with these big, slow strides, just like the Undertaker, and I'd run around like a madman trying to avoid his grasp.

One thing that carried over from my living room wrestling career into my school life was all the acting.

The classroom at School 21 was my stage. I liked social studies, and I remember memorizing all the presidents in fifth-grade U.S. history. But the classroom *setting* was what I really thrived on.

MY MOTHER WOULD ALWAYS ENCOURAGE ME TO TRY NEW THINGS.

Every day, there'd be thirty-five people in the audience, including the teacher, and I'd take the opportunity to perform. I'd watch TV shows like *Martin* and *Family Matters* and reenact my favorite scenes in class.

I had a natural curiosity to dive into things and explore. My mother would always encourage me to try new things. One of them—maybe my darkest secret that absolutely nobody knows—was playing the flute.

Yes, I played the flute.

I was in the fourth grade. In music class we had to choose an instrument to play for the entire school year. My friends all picked the more "manly" ones, like the trombone or the trumpet. But all the cute girls in my class chose the flute. That seemed like a good reason to give it a shot.

I brought that little silver flute, tucked away in its brown case, everywhere I went. The older kids on the block made fun of me, but I was the only boy who played the flute that year, so I was the center of attention. What more could a ten-year-old kid ask for?

My mother worked very hard to provide for us. She was always on the move, often pulling double shifts and working overtime to pay the bills. Once I got a little bit older, she put me into the YMCA after-school program. We did it all there. We swam in the pool, we played tag, and we did gymnastics. I was always competitive. If we were doing cartwheels, I'd make sure my form was the best. If we were holding our breaths under water, I'd almost pass out trying to hold my breath the longest. I loved all the activities at the Y, but they were just hobbies, things to do.

My first *real* passion? The ancient art of tae kwon do.

THE SECOND FLOOR of 44 East Twentieth Street was the home of Manny Quiles's tae kwon do studio. I didn't know Manny Quiles's real name at the time. To me, he was always "The Sir."

The Sir's studio was one story below our apartment. At all hours of the day, I'd watch older kids shuffle up and down the stairwell in their white robes. I was always curious about what went on down there, but my mother said I was far too young for martial arts. Finally, when I was seven, my curiosity about the action downstairs got the better of her.

The Sir was probably in his late thirties or early forties, but he could have run a marathon or fought a tiger on a day's notice. He was Colombian with a grayish crew cut, and he was always in his white robe, barefoot.

The Sir's dojo was covered in floor-to-ceiling mirrors, and it had an unforgettable smell of sweat and socks. We had classes three days a week, and when you arrived, you entered his world for that entire hour. No talking, no goofing off, and no horsing around.

I dove right into tae kwon do. I loved the discipline and the focus. There were also clearly defined, tangible goals. We had tests every three or four months, and I'd study for them for hours. The test was more than sparring with opponents and winning matches. We also had five-page paper packets to memorize. There was a ton of information on those sheets—the history of tae kwon do, the great masters, all the different moves and positions. To pass The Sir's tests, you had to know it all. We would do sparring, we would do our pattern, and then we lined up in front of a panel of judges.

The panel was made up of The Sir, a senior black belt named Garfield, and an old Asian man that we all just referred to as "The O.G." He was probably sixty-five years old, but he was a ninth-degree black belt and could still do a spinning hook kick that'd knock your butt on the canvas.

He was like a mythical figure to us. I'm not sure how, but he had the 411 on everyone. He'd come prepared with personal questions about everyone. I always looked forward to my time with The O.G., but a lot of my friends would choke and blow it on test days solely because of his haunting presence.

I went from a yellow belt to a green belt, then to a blue, and to a red. The red belt is the belt before the ultimate honor—the black belt. I never wanted anything more than that black belt. I'd walk around the house in my robe, practicing moves and reciting the tenets of tae kwon do. By the time I stood up in front of the panel, with a black belt on the line, I was a Martial Arts Encyclopedia. I was ready for any question the panel could possibly ask.

I stood there, my head spinning with information.

"Victor, congratulations," said The Sir.

"What? There's no test?" I had prepared for months. I was ready for the toughest test of my life.

"There's no test," he said. "With your commitment and determination over the past few years, you've already proved to us that you're worthy."

It was an incredible moment and an incredible honor. According to The Sir, at twelve years old I was the youngest tae kwon do black belt in New Jersey state history.

Tae kwon do opened up new doors for me. I got to travel across the country, performing in showcases and tournaments. I took tae kwon do very seriously, but I always remembered that regardless of how heated the competition, it was supposed to be fun. From The Sir, I learned the importance of preparedness. If you came prepared, no matter what the situation, you could never be caught off guard.

I would never have met The Sir had we not lived one floor above his dojo. That's how life works sometimes. You're just in the right place at the right time. You're put in situations where you have the opportunity to better yourself.

After I earned my black belt, I decided to quit tae kwon do. It was time to try something new.

Two years later, The Sir's daughter earned her black belt at the age of ten.

I wasn't too upset. After all, records are made to be broken.

ONE DAY WHEN I was seven years old, I was eating in the kitchen when I heard a commotion outside our front door. I poked my head out into the hallway and saw my mother speaking with a tall African-American man in a T-shirt and blue jeans. Who was this guy? I'd never seen him in my life.

His name was Mike Walker.

He was my father.

Mike Walker met my mother at a bus stop in Paterson in 1982. He threw some pickup lines at her, and though she thought he was handsome, she deflected his compliments at first. She was on her way to work and wasn't interested in being hit on at seven a.m. But he wouldn't give up. When he offered her a ride to work in his car, so she wouldn't have to take the bus, she finally said yes. When they discovered that they both shared the same birthday—March 1—just one year apart, a connection was made.

They began seeing each other soon thereafter. A firefighter in Paterson, Mike Walker had hours that were always changing. They'd go out here and there, enjoying each other's company.

After four years of an on-again, off-again courtship, my mother discovered that she was pregnant. When she told Mike the news, he wasn't thrilled.

His reaction wasn't a shock to my mother. She was aware that he already had a wife and two kids living nearby.

Mike told her that with another family to provide for, he wasn't sure how big a role he'd be able to play in this new child's life. Things got rocky. When she told him she was keeping her baby, he walked away.

On November 11, 1986, Victor Cruz—all nine pounds, three ounces—was born at Barnert Hospital in Paterson.

As a little kid, I don't remember ever asking who my father was or feeling bad about not having him around. None of my friends on the block really had fathers either. That's just the way it was. We all had strong single mothers who cared, loved, and provided for us.

Then, in 1993, my father showed up. I'll never know exactly why, but something inside him, seven years after the fact, had spurred him to take responsibility for his actions.

IT WAS COOL HAVING A DAD. I NEVER RESENTED HIM.

I initially resisted. My life was good as it was. I remember thinking, Who does this guy think he is?

But that didn't last too long. It was cool having a dad.

I never resented him. I'm sure my mother could have used his help earlier, and I know the pain he must have caused her. I also know he wasn't proud of the way he handled the situation. He was ashamed. It took a real man to recognize his wrongs and try to make up for them.

My mother and father never got back together, but they got along. He lived one town over in Passaic and often came around. Dad had two other children—Ebony and Malik—and he brought me into their lives. He'd refer to Malik as my brother and Ebony as my sister. Though we didn't have the same mothers, the three of us were family.

My dad wanted to have a role in my life; he wanted to love me as a son. My mother could have denied him that opportunity, but she didn't. My mom's an incredible woman. Of all her great virtues, the fact that she was able to embrace Mike Walker entering my life is one of the things I'm most thankful for. If it took a courageous man to knock on that door and say he wanted to meet me seven years after turning his back on my existence, it took an even stronger woman to say yes and grant him that honor.

Dad would come by three or four times a week and we gradually developed a real father-and-son relationship. I was in awe of his career as a firefighter and the courage it took to do his job. I'd get scared when I'd hear the fire truck sirens at night, imagining that he'd be forced into a dangerous situation. When I'd see him the next day, I'd always be relieved that he was okay.

When I was about ten years old, he plopped me in front of the TV and told me to watch something I'd never really seen before. It was an NFL game. The San Francisco 49ers were playing the Detroit Lions. Football was a little tricky to follow at first, but I remember the cameras always focusing on one guy—number 80 in white and red. His name was Jerry Rice.

Despite not knowing the rules of the game, I could tell that this guy was very special because he was the only player any of the announcers were talking about.

Giants Stadium was just fifteen miles away from Paterson, but I had no allegiance to either the Giants or the Jets (who shared the stadium). Instead, I quickly became a fan of the 49ers and the Giants' shared rival—the Dallas Cowboys.

Those mid-1990s Cowboys teams had it all. The big personalities, the cheerleaders, the winning tradition. Emmitt Smith was the ultimate running back. My father would tell me to watch how Smith used his blockers and handled himself on the field. You never saw Emmitt Smith lose his cool or turn the ball over. "Why does he run it up the middle all the time?" I'd ask anxiously. "Why doesn't he just run to the outside away from all the defenders?" My father would explain the importance of the offensive line, and how just because a running back had the ball in his hands, it was still an eleven-man effort.

And then there was Deion.

Deion Sanders was something else! More than being the best cornerback and punt return man in the game,

Deion had personality and a unique style. He was a true showman. He wore these great bandannas and would do his signature high-step move every time he had the ball in the open field.

That 1995 Dallas Cowboys team was the first NFL squad I followed on a weekly basis. They went 12-4, breezed through the NFC playoffs, and beat the Pittsburgh Steelers in the Super Bowl. My mother bought me a Deion Sanders number 21 jersey, the one with the stars on the shoulders. I wore that thing *every day*. For my birthday that year, Ebony, who was six years older than I was, bought me a children's book about a little boy who aspired to play in the NFL. It had my name in it, and drawings of a boy overcoming all sorts of obstacles to make it to the big leagues. I loved that book and read it every night.

Two years after I watched my first football game on TV, my father asked me if I wanted to actually *play* football on a team. I'd been "playing" football in the street with my friends for a few years, but this was different. This would be real, full-impact, tackle football.

My mother wasn't so keen on me playing because of the physicality of the sport, but she left it up to me. When my father asked, "Are you going to play on the PAL North Firefighters or what?" I looked at her for guidance. She just shrugged, and said, "You're a big boy. It's up to you."

FINDING
STABILITY

M Y MOTHER WOULD later tell me that one of the reasons she allowed me to play football was because it would keep me occupied after school.

I rep Paterson with a tremendous amount of pride, but it's not all roses and rainbows. When I was eleven years old, I missed the bus one day and had to walk home from School 21. It's a short, three-block walk, and my mother had told me to walk straight down Madison Avenue to East Twentieth Street.

I'd always been told not to walk down Broadway alone. By the late nineties, it had become dangerous. But that day I thought it'd be quicker. I got scared, though, seeing the older men lining the streets. An overall feeling of hopelessness hung over them.

I kept on walking, thinking I'd be home soon enough.

Out of the shadows, a man grabbed me by my shirt collar. He was older and stank of cheap liquor. Initially, I panicked, but he told me to calm down. "Chill out, little man. It's all good. Where are you headed?"

I told him I was going to my grandmother's house, and that I was lost. Maybe he could help me find my way.

I was young and naïve. He was drunk.

He mumbled something and handed me a half-smoked joint. I'd never gotten high before, let alone smelled marijuana. "Take a hit, little man. Breathe in, and then blow it out."

DANGER WAS ALWAYS LURKING.

I refused. He was persistent, and when I kept refusing, his tone changed. "You've got to take a hit or you're never getting home," he said, tightening his hold on my shirt.

It was a terrible situation. I didn't think. I just acted. In one motion, I grabbed the joint, threw it to the ground, turned around, and ran back to Madison Avenue. I sprinted to a nearby pay phone. When I got ahold of my mother at work, I was crying. She had my grandfather come get me and take me home.

My grandfather always said, "If your life is stable, the rest will fall into place." But life in Paterson wasn't stable on its own. You had to work hard to *make* it stable.

Danger was always lurking. In elementary and middle school, there was always a fistfight or a brawl of some sort during recess or lunch.

I was no angel myself. I remember one day when a boy got a pass to wear his hat in school because he had gotten a terrible haircut the day before. The second we got out of first period, I went right up to him and ripped that hat off his head.

His haircut really was awful.

Another time, there was a kid a few years older who took my seat in homeroom. He was twice my size, but I wasn't about to let some goon steal my chair. When he got up for the Pledge of Allegiance, I snuck up behind him and moved his chair five feet to the left. When he went to sit down, he fell flat on his butt. The entire class was in hysterics, but he didn't find it too funny. He got mad and wanted to fight me after school. I'm pretty sure we did.

One afternoon, my friends and I were playing pickup basketball at Montgomery Park. Five on five. I was never a big talker on the court. I tried to let my game speak for itself. But my boy Pelli was a different story. He was the rapper in our crew of friends, and he was always running his mouth. We were playing against five Dominican kids, and I was just lighting it up. I couldn't miss a shot. After every basket, Pelli would get in the face of the kid covering me. "You can't hold my boy! You're terrible! We're eating you alive!" The boy got more and more physical with me on defense, and whenever Pelli would start shouting in his face, he'd answer with a shove or a stare.

After we won, the kid who was covering me came up to Pelli and told us to meet him in the parking lot.

Pelli and I shrugged it off. We figured whatever happened on the court stayed on the court. We were just having fun.

After the game, my mom was supposed to pick us up in her van. But before she got there, we found the kid waiting for us. Only, he wasn't alone. Twenty of his friends were there with him. Some were our age, but others were older. They all wore matching bandannas, and a few were holding baseball bats and bottles.

Pelli and I looked at each other. I remember asking him, "Pelli, what the hell's about to go down here?"

And Pelli, always the talker, looked back at me. "Vic, shit's about to go down."

I was like, "Vic?! You were the one talking all that smack, not me!" But Pelli was my boy, and if "shit" was about to go down, I wasn't letting him go at it alone.

We both took off our backpacks and jackets. Then we put up our fists. The first wave of kids rushed forward, six of them for each of us. We threw punches, doing our best to stay on our feet. At one point we managed to start running down the block. One kid in particular chased after me.

He got closer and closer.

I slowed down and, without even thinking about it, broke out a move that The Sir must have taught me. I leaped in the air, spun around, and punched the boy square in the nose.

I'd never punched another person in the face like that. There was blood every-where. The boy, probably two or three years older than me, cried out. "You broke my nose!" he screamed.

I'D NEVER PUNCHED ANOTHER PERSON IN THE FACE LIKE THAT.

I kept running. Suddenly, I remembered that I had left my new North Face jacket behind in the parking lot. I loved that jacket. I knew how hard my mother had worked to buy it. Losing it over a silly fight was terribly irresponsible.

At that instant, my mother's blue minivan came flying by. Pelli was already inside, and he pulled the door open. I hopped in, out of breath, and looked at him. His face was all bruised and bleeding. He'd gotten beaten up pretty badly.

But he had my jacket in his hands.

MY MOTHER AND I moved out of my *abuela* and *Papi*'s apartment after my sister Andrea was born. Our new spot, on the corner of East Eighteenth Street, was slightly bigger than our old digs. I still had my own room, but we also had a front yard that I could play in and a big basement downstairs. When my friends came over for sleepovers, we'd play hide-and-seek and capture the flag. I spent endless hours slam-dunking a miniature NERF basketball off the wood paneling that lined the ceiling.

Being a big brother took some getting used to. I had always been my mother's little angel, her one and only. When Andrea was born, all that changed. I'd be off in the corner, doing a crazy back flip or showing off my latest tae kwon do moves, and instead of watching me, Mom would be busy with Andrea, pinching her cheeks or fussing over something cute she said. But after I saw how much my little sister looked up to me, I enjoyed having her around.

Though just two streets over from my old home, East Eighteenth was much lonelier. On East Twentieth, all of my friends lived in the houses next door. It was a one-way street, and we played outside all the time without cars ever really bothering us. There was an old run-down house at the end of East Twentieth that we all said was haunted. The windows were boarded up, and you could smell it from the street. I'll never forget that stench. It was like a rotting corpse.

None of us had ever dared step foot in that house.

One year on Halloween, though, we all agreed that we'd walk through the front door. It would be our rite of passage, the night the boys of East Twentieth Street would all become men.

Alex was first, and there was a line of us about six deep behind him. He took one step inside the house.

Silence.

The next two or three seconds felt like hours.

Then Alex let out the shrillest scream. "Ghost! I see a ghost!"

He ran past the rest of us faster than we had ever seen him run before. We followed him, screaming, tripping all over each other in the middle of the street.

Maybe we weren't ready to be "men" just yet.

Living on East Eighteenth was very different in other ways too. Our new house was on one of the busiest and noisiest corners in Paterson. Sometimes the noise was great. The guys on the corner would blast the latest Biggie or Jay-Z song from their boom boxes even before the album had dropped. The sound of the ice cream man's truck on a hot summer day always brought a smile to my face too.

But many nights I'd be in bed, trying to sleep, and I'd hear the sound of gunshots. Sometimes they were far off in the distance. Other times they were much closer. Once, I heard gunshots so loud that they felt like they were going off right inside my house.

They weren't, but that fear of seeing something horrible—or God forbid, having something horrible happen to Andrea, my mother, or me—was always present. With-

35

out *Papí* or my father living with us, I was the man of the house. For a young kid in Paterson, that was an incredible burden to carry.

A FEW YEARS after we moved, I got to see the home-land of José Feliciano and the extended Cruz family when we took a vacation to Puerto Rico. After a few days in Old San Juan, we went to Arecibo, the small Puerto Rican town where my *abuela* had grown up

We'd be sitting having lunch on my uncle Victor's porch and little wild horses would be running below us on the sand. I'd been to the Jersey Shore a few times as a little kid, but the beaches in Jersey didn't hold a candle to the ones in Puerto Rico.

Every morning, we were woken up at six o'clock.

Not by an alarm clock, but by roosters. No lie, *roosters*.

"Cock-a-doodle-doo!" I thought they only made that noise in the cartoons, but it was real. And you didn't just roll over and ignore a rooster. Once they got started, you were up for the rest of the day.

I LEARNED A LOT ABOUT MY PUERTO RICAN HERITAGE ON THAT TRIP.

I learned a lot about my Puerto Rican heritage on that trip.

My *abuela* had always cooked the most amazing arroz con pollo and empanadas in her kitchen. And the sounds of the Spanish guitar, the merengue, and the salsa had been the soundtrack of my youth. But until I actually went to Puerto Rico and saw its beauty with my very own eyes, I didn't feel truly connected to the native land of my mother and my *abuela*.

There were very few Puerto Ricans in the NBA or the NFL when I was little. I always noticed that. You never saw players with Hispanic last names dunking basketballs or hauling in touchdown passes. I wanted to change that someday.

I didn't know what sport I'd end up playing. But I couldn't wait to have a team's name on the front of my jersey and the word *Cruz* written on the back.

CHAPTER 3

A FIREFIGHTER'S SON

WHEN I WAS in seventh or eighth grade, I read a book about Larry Bird, the great Boston Celtics forward. Bird had grown up in a small town in Indiana called French Lick. I always loved that name. He ended up taking Indiana State to the finals of the 1979 NCAA Tournament. Larry Bird was the pride of French Lick. There was a picture in that book of a giant green sign, shaped like a basketball, on a main road in French Lick. The sign read *Larry Bird Blvd*. He had a street named after him.

Tim Thomas was Paterson's version of Larry Bird. Hundreds of great athletes had grown up in Paterson, but for one reason or another, none of them seemed to ever make it. You'd hear about a football star recruited by a Big 10 school, only to fall in with the wrong crowd or break a leg and never leave town.

Tim Thomas was different in more ways than one. He was the rare big man who played like a guard. In 1995, his senior year at Paterson Catholic, he averaged twenty-five points and fifteen rebounds per game. Everyone in

Paterson knew about Tim Thomas. Everyone in Paterson *loved* Tim Thomas.

Thomas was also the rare athlete from our city who had held the world at his fingertips and *didn't* piss it away. There were no criminal charges, no unfortunate incidents, and no devastating injuries. He was a McDonald's All-American, the ultimate honor for a high school basketball player, and got recruited by just about every big school in the country. When he chose to go to Villanova, outside Philadelphia, we all became Villanova fans overnight. And when he started playing for the Philadelphia 76ers, the 76ers became the unofficial NBA team of Paterson, New Jersey.

Thomas was smooth in the NBA, playing fourteen seasons in the pros. My father would tell me, "Keep it up. Keep studying, keep playing, and keep surrounding yourself with the right people. You can make it. Just look at Tim Thomas."

Thomas's high school coach at Paterson Catholic had been a man named Jim Salmon. My father and Mr. Salmon were very friendly. Working for the city as a firefighter, and being involved in so many Little Leagues and sports programs, my dad was one of those guys who knew just about everyone.

Dad introduced me to Jim Salmon at a young age, and he took a liking to me. In his eyes, I played basketball the right way. Though I could shoot well and jump high, I always got a thrill out of bringing the ball up the court and making the right pass. I was always diving for loose balls, scraping my knees, and fighting to give my team another possession.

With some needling from my father, Jim invited me to play for his Amateur Athletic Union—AAU—team. After Tim Thomas had made it to the NBA, he and Mr. Salmon had started up a traveling basketball team from our area. Our team name? The Tim Thomas Playaz.

Every kid in Paterson wanted to be on the Playaz. I was one of the youngest guys, but got some serious playing time as a point guard. My job wasn't to score thirty points a game. My job was to put my teammates in the best positions possible for success.

When I finished the eighth grade and graduated from School 21, I was supposed to attend Eastside High School. One of the two big public high schools in Paterson, Eastside was made famous by the 1989 movie *Lean on Me*. In that film, principal Joe Clark, played by Morgan Freeman, shapes up a violent, out-of-control student body. He uses radical methods of discipline, like locking the children in the classroom and dangling troublesome ones over rooftops.

It's a great film and a true story, but Eastside hardly became some perfect school after that movie came out. It was located on Park Avenue, and Park Avenue was tough.

On that street corner, right outside the school, drug dealers and gang members were always posting up. The school was massive too. There must have been twenty-five hundred kids at Eastside.

Though many of my friends were going there, my mother suggested I attend Passaic County Technical Institute, which was one town over. Academically, Tech had a better reputation than Eastside, and athletically, they were far superior. My mother also knew there was a much smaller chance of me finding trouble at Tech. To get in, I had to write a thousand-word essay on why I wanted to go there. I took a lot of pride in that essay, explaining how I could make a better life for myself at Tech. And the hard work paid off. I was accepted and I was on my way.

But when I first got to Tech, it was overwhelming. My freshman year was my first time in a big school setting. Though not as big as Eastside, Tech still had three hundred students in each grade. The school was physically enormous too. There were floors, floors, and more floors.

And I took advantage.

Instead of raising my hand or taking a leadership role in the classroom, I'd ask if I could use the bathroom. And then I'd go on walks. Like, really long walks. I'd stroll the halls for ten minutes, twenty minutes, thirty minutes. I'd do laps around the school, popping my head into random classrooms and causing trouble.

Academics were no longer a priority. I'd get B's and C's, and when my mother said, "You should be doing better than this, Victor," I'd just shrug it off. "B's and C's are fine," I'd tell her. I figured if I wasn't failing out of school, I was in the clear.

Athletically, I played on the freshman football team and had a good season. It was the first year Tech had fielded a freshman football squad, and we only played four games. I enjoyed it, but basketball remained my true love.

Tech wasn't a traditional basketball powerhouse, but there were two kids a year ahead of me who brought the school some national recognition. Darryl Watkins was seven feet tall when he was thirteen years old. By the time he was a sophomore, he was one of the top thirty high school basketball players in the entire country. His nickname was "Mookie," and he was unstoppable in the paint. One of Mookie's best friends on the team was Colin Bailey. Colin wasn't quite the dominant player that Mookie was, but he had a silky-smooth jump shot and could run the court. Though I started the season on the junior varsity team, I befriended them both. We had a real chemistry on the court during practice. I'd play point guard, Colin would play forward, and Mookie would be the center.

Tech's archrival was Paterson Catholic. It was a powerhouse in New Jersey sports, a private school known for sending Tim Thomas to Villanova and the pros. That season, we traveled to Paterson Catholic's gym to play them in a highly anticipated battle.

It was the first time I'd played in front of a large crowd. I thrived on the energy in the gym. Sometimes in sports, you enter this place called "The Zone." You're not supposed to acknowledge when you're in The Zone. But when it happens, you can't be stopped. That day, I was in The Zone. I scored twenty-seven points, and had ten assists. It was just the JV game, but we upset Paterson Catholic, and a lot of important basketball people were in the crowd. College scouts were there to watch Mookie and Colin, but so was Tommy Patterson, the head coach of Paterson Catholic. After the game, he patted me on the head and said he was very impressed with my play.

Mookie, Colin, and the rest of the varsity guys got the best of Paterson Catholic's varsity team that evening. It was a great day for Tech, but I left that gym knowing that someday I wanted to be a part of the Paterson Catholic tradition.

I finished the season averaging twenty points per game

for the JV team and suited up for a few Varsity games down the stretch. Things were going great on the court, but they were only getting worse in the classroom. Those B's and C's from before were becoming C's and D's. My behavior in the classroom wasn't much better. I was cocky, girls were starting to notice me, and people I'd never even met—adults—were telling me how good I was at basketball. It was all starting to go to my head.

That's when Jim Salmon stepped in.

I got home from school one day in late February of 2001 and found Jim seated in the living room with my mother and father. Jim had never been in my house before.

Something was up.

"I'm taking you on a trip," Jim said sternly. "Just the two of us."

Where were we going? I had no idea.

"Pack a bag for two days and two nights, and grab a snack for the road. We're taking a flight," he said. My parents nodded in agreement. Clearly, they had told Jim how much I was struggling in school.

So I packed a duffel bag and hopped in Jim's car. When we got to the airport, I was handed a plane ticket. Destination: Raleigh, North Carolina.

"You're coming with me on a trip that could change your life," Jim said. "I want to introduce you to some people and show you some things."

A life-changing trip, huh? I buckled my seat belt on the plane and imagined the very worst.

When we landed, we rented a car and drove to a nearby town called Durham. It was the last week in February, but the weather was perfect. And everything was so . . . green.

We took a right turn on to a long, willowy road and saw beautiful buildings and students dressed in all blue.

"Welcome to Duke." Jim smiled.

Duke? Like Christian Laettner, Grant Hill, Coach K Duke? I pinched myself. My whole life, Duke basketball was right up there on my Mount Rushmore of sports with the Dallas Cowboys, Chicago Bulls, and, well, Tim Thomas.

We pulled up to an apartment complex and a familiar face from high school and college basketball games on TV came out the front door.

"Jim! What took you so long, man?" asked Dahntay Jones, a six-foot-six small forward from Trenton, New Jersey.

"Dahntay, I want you to meet Victor Cruz. He's a young, up-and-coming point guard from Paterson." Jim had known Dahntay from AAU basketball and was one of the positive male role models in *his* life.

Dahntay put his arm around Jim's shoulder. "If this guy says you're good," Dahntay said, smiling, "you must be pretty good."

That night, Coach Salmon, Dahntay, and I went to dinner at one of the fancier restaurants in Durham. It was unbelievable. Students and parents kept coming over to welcome Dahntay to Duke and tell him how excited they were to have him there for next season.

Midway through our dinner, another familiar-looking person came walking over. "Jim Salmon, in the flesh! When I heard you were in town, I had to come by." It was North Carolina's star shooting guard, Joe Forte, the reigning ACC Men's Basketball Rookie of the Year.

All night Dahntay and Joe spoke to me like big brothers. They told me how important it was for me to treat the classroom as seriously as I treated the basketball court.

"There were guys just as good as me during my freshman year of high school," said Forte, a high school hoops legend from Maryland. "But a lot of those kids ran into trouble or their bad grades kept them from making it to the next level. Don't be one of those guys."

Dahntay took particular interest in my studies. "What are you doing after practice? Are you going home and studying? Or are you meeting up with your friends and screwing around? Get your schoolwork in order and the rest will follow, man. College coaches won't even look at you if you're flunking out of high school."

The next day, Jim and I sat in the parents' section at Cameron Indoor Stadium for a game Duke was playing against the University of Virginia. That place was huge, like the Paterson Catholic gym on steroids. When the game started, I recognized another familiar face on the court. Donald Hand was Virginia's captain. I'd seen him play point guard on the Eastside Park courts most of my life. He was a Paterson Catholic graduate and starting for the Cavaliers. Jim pointed to Donald. "Everyone talks about Tim Thomas in Paterson, but I'm almost just as proud of Donald's accomplishments. He's going to graduate from the University of Virginia with a degree in anthropology."

Duke blew out Virginia that night. After the game, Donald Hand came running over to give Jim a huge hug. He'd known Coach Salmon his entire life. Jim told Donald that I was a young player from Paterson, and Hand looked me right in the eye. "Always be proud of where you came from," he said very seriously. "Always be sure to represent Paterson with class and dignity. You're next in line, man. Do Paterson proud."

It was all such an incredible experience. I couldn't wipe the smile off my face for weeks. My friends, some of whom were already getting involved with gangs and drugs at Eastside High, couldn't believe me when I told them about my weekend.

But the basketball wasn't what stuck with me. Donald Hand, Joe Forte, and Dahntay Jones weren't lucky. They had worked hard to get where they were, both on the basketball court and off.

The trip to North Carolina motivated me to get my act together. In the last two quarters of my freshman year, I got all A's and B's.

I also started to look into transferring to Paterson Catholic.

AFTER MY FRESHMAN season, Mookie, Colin, and I started talking about our futures at Tech. They were both big-time high school basketball stars. They had been thinking long and hard about it and, though they liked Tech, they wanted to transfer to Paterson Catholic. I wanted to go with them.

It was a tricky situation.

There was a lot of excitement at Tech about the basketball program after that 2000–2001 season. Tech actually had a better squad than Paterson Catholic. If all three of us left, we'd cripple the team.

I'd made some friends at school, but I had always wanted to play for the Paterson Catholic Cougars. I'd wanted to go where Tim Thomas went as a little kid, and now, having met Donald Hand in Durham, I really wanted to go where he went.

More important, PC suited me better in the classroom. The classes at Tech were enormous, and there wasn't much keeping me from roaming the halls all day. At Paterson Catholic, every student was accounted for. After my mother agreed (and came up with the money to pay for private school), it was a done deal.

Or so I thought.

If it had just been me—five-foot-eight Victor Cruz, point guard on the Passaic County Technical Institute's junior varsity basketball squad—nobody would have blinked an eye at my transfer. But Darryl Watkins was a seven-foot basketball prodigy. Colin Bailey had college scouts watching his every game. When all three of us filed transfer forms at the same time, a controversy erupted.

The New Jersey State Interscholastic Athletic Association, a nonprofit organization sanctioned by the state to oversee high school athletics, cried foul. The NJSIAA denied our transfer requests. Why? They said our transfers were illegitimate because we were only going to Paterson Catholic for "athletic reasons."

So we took the organization to court.

Because Darryl was such a high-profile athlete, there was media coverage in all the newspapers for weeks. Traditionally, the NJSIAA ruled with an iron fist, and their decisions were rarely challenged. But in our case the judge only needed a few hours to declare that the association's rules were "vague and ambiguous." Its penalties were "arbitrary, capricious, and unreasonable."

Mookie, Colin, and I were going to be Paterson Catholic Cougars after all.

The court case kept me from practicing with the football team over the summer, so I couldn't join the squad. I wanted to play, but I'd have to wait another year. Who needed football, though? I was looking forward to becoming the next great point guard at Paterson Catholic.

That first week of my sophomore year was pure bliss. I loved wearing that Paterson Catholic maroon sweater every day. I dove into my studies and actually found myself enjoying the subjects. With just twenty kids in each class, I felt like the teachers cared about each one of us.

At Paterson Catholic, every school day started with homeroom. At eight a.m., you came in and got settled in your assigned classroom. There was a TV in every classroom turned to channel 1, an educational station that only airs in schools. No one really ever paid attention. But on Tuesday morning my second week of school, a few of the students noticed some weird images being shown on channel 1.

Over and over again, the same visuals were repeated—two different planes crashing into New York City's World Trade Center. At first I thought we were watching a sneak preview or a trailer to some new disaster movie. But soon it became evident that this was no fictional film.

If you were to ask me about any other day of my soph-omore year of high school, I couldn't tell you much. But I remember every minute of 9/11 as if it were yesterday.

Instead of everyone going to first period, Sister Glo-ria, the principal at Paterson Catholic, called us all to the auditorium. She explained that New York City had been attacked, and that we'd be having an early dismissal. She advised us to go directly home and connect with our par-ents and loved ones as soon as we left the school grounds.

I was young, though, and it just didn't seem like what I had seen on TV had any *real* impact on me personally. So, I didn't go right home. I went and played basketball at the park with my friends.

At around two p.m., I checked my cell phone. There were twenty-five missed calls from my mother.

Twenty-five.

I called her immediately. She was out of breath, simul-taneously screaming and crying, "Victor, where have you been?"

I told her that I'd been at the park, just playing basket-ball. Why she was so upset?

When I got home, the gravity of the situation became a lot clearer. I watched the coverage on the television, and I saw the faces of those New Yorkers running through the clouds of smoke. I discovered that this wasn't just a freak accident on a random Tuesday in September. It was a calculated attack, not only on New York but Washington, D.C., too. Thousands of Americans, who had gone to work that Tuesday just as they would have on any other day, would never go home again.

Many of those individuals were firefighters.

I thought of my father, a Paterson firefighter for more than two decades.

Then I thought of the children of all the innocent people killed in the attacks.

I got ahold of my father on the phone. He let me know that he was safe and sound, but that a lot of good men and women had been lost that day. I didn't sleep that night, thinking about him, thinking about life, and thinking of how the New York City skyline was forever changed.

The next morning the sound of a phone ringing woke us early. It was my father. He told me that he was heading down to Ground Zero. He explained that he felt it was his duty as a firefighter to volunteer and help those in need.

I was scared.

Was it safe? What if there was another attack? What if parts of the damaged buildings fell on him while he was helping out?

My father spent the next five days at Ground Zero, volunteering his services. He'd call us every night, but he'd never give us any details on what he saw.

After 9/11, I had a new appreciation for my father

and his life's work. Whenever I think of that iconic image of the firemen putting up the American flag amidst the rubble of Ground Zero, I get goose bumps. My father was one of those brave men.

I also had a new sense of connection to New York City.

The entire country bonded together during that time, but New Jersey and New York got even closer. New York was no longer this distant, far-off dream world. New York and New Jersey were one.

TRYING SOMETHING NEW

PATERSON CATHOLIC HAD everything I was looking for in a high school. My grades immediately improved because I found the classes interesting. The teachers cared about us too. Sister Gloria was always concerned with my well-being. She turned out to be a tough cookie with a heart of gold.

I played point guard for the varsity basketball team, and we had a phenomenal season. Mookie and Colin had gotten even better in their junior years, but we also had an electric shooting guard named Marquis Webb. He and I made for a dynamic backcourt duo.

We won the county championship that year, but the real highlight of that season for me was a game against Don Bosco Tech. They weren't a very good team, but their starting point guard was none other than Malik Walker.

Yes, my older brother, Malik.

My father did his very best to attend all of our games, regardless of the sport, and you always *knew* when Mike Walker was in the stands. My dad was the one scream-ing at the referee from the bleachers about a bad call or razzing an opposing coach for a bad decision. One time he got so heated over an officiating mistake that he was physically removed from the premises. I probably should have been embarrassed, but I remember laughing the entire time as the security guards took him out. He had been right! The call was terrible.

Malik was a solid player. He had a nice jump shot and good court sense. We played one-on-one a lot as kids, and he'd always beat me. Physically, he was just stronger, and he'd bully me inside.

When I turned thirteen, that all changed.

We blew Don Bosco Tech out of the building that afternoon. Coach Patterson drew up all sorts of isolation plays for me, and I had a blast, scoring a few buckets right over Malik. Our whole team cheered me on from the bench and even Malik had a good laugh at the "Victor vs. Malik" strategy that Coach Patterson employed.

My father had shown up an hour early. He was as nervous as I'd ever seen him. But he didn't say a word the entire game. He had told both Malik and me that he wouldn't be "choosing sides." He also promised himself he'd be quiet. My mother laughed at that one, saying, "That was the only game where I didn't hear your dad's voice in the background from start to finish."

That following summer, I traveled the country with the Tim Thomas Playaz. Jim took us to some of the top AAU tournaments, and we faced off against elite basketball players from all over America.

Meanwhile, back in Paterson, things weren't going as well for some of my old friends. During my sophomore year alone, four of them became fathers. Several of the girls I'd innocently flirted with in the cafeteria just two years earlier were now young, single mothers. Some kids I'd known stopped showing up in Montgomery Park to play basketball. I'd find out later that they were in jail or, worse, no longer alive.

It was very easy to fall into bad situations in Paterson. You didn't have to find them. They would find you.

I avoided that trouble, which is a testament to my mother. Throughout high school, my mother worked full days and overtime hours. Still, she would always be waiting for me outside the YMCA or the Willowbrook Mall at nine thirty at night. She tried her best to be at every game, every team dinner, and every trophy presentation.

My mom was meddlesome when she felt she had to be—I'm sure my high

IT WAS VERY EASY TO FALL INTO BAD SITUATIONS IN PATERSON. YOU DIDN'T HAVE TO FIND THEM. THEY WOULD FIND YOU.

school girlfriends didn't always appreciate that—and she always needed to know exactly where I was. I'd get annoyed when she'd yell at me for not calling her *the second* I got home from school.

Now I'm forever grateful for that.

Mom didn't need to be everywhere, though, and some of the best times I had in high school were at a place called Skaters World.

Yes, Skaters World.

It was a roller-skating rink up in Wayne, a suburban town about fifteen minutes north of Paterson.

On Friday nights, Pelli, my friend Kyon, and I would get dressed in our best clothes, drench ourselves in Versace Blue Jeans cologne, and get a ride to Wayne.

We'd arrive at Skaters World around eight thirty. I don't recall ever actually renting a pair of roller skates. We'd just set up shop in a corner and hang out. I'd be sporting my leather Paterson Catholic varsity basketball jacket, the one with *County Champions* embroidered in fur on the back, and *Vic* in cursive on the front. There were packs of girls from all the neighboring schools milling around. We'd get slices of pizza, drink soda, and do our best to look like we knew what the hell we were doing.

At eleven, the nights took off.

The DJ, a charismatic dude named Big L, would take the microphone and urge everyone to "get on the rink."

Big L played the hottest music. We'd dance our faces off. I'd sweat more on that dance floor than I ever did in a basketball game. We'd have a blast out there, getting girls' numbers and acting like big shots.

My mom wasn't crazy about me coming in at one in the morning, but she slept better knowing that there were worse places I could be than a roller-skating rink in Wayne, New Jersey.

ONE AFTERNOON DURING the summer before my junior year, my father asked me if I was going to play football for Paterson Catholic that fall.

I liked football, and still followed my Dallas Cowboys on Sundays. But I hadn't really considered playing for Paterson Catholic.

"You should play football, Vic," he told me. "You're pretty good."

Dad was always my biggest fan on the gridiron. And the idea intrigued me. At the very least, I figured, football would keep me physically active until basketball season.

When I spoke to the football coach, Mr. Wimberly, he was open to me joining the squad.

"I'll tell you now, though,

"YOU SHOULD PLAY FOOTBALL, VIC," HE TOLD ME. "YOU'RE PRETTY GOOD."

Victor," he said, "football's a whole lot different than basketball."

Truer words had never been spoken.

When I showed up for my first Paterson Catholic football practice that August, there were about eighty-five kids on the football field. They all had their own football vocabulary and set positions. Having not played real, organized football in three years, I was overwhelmed.

The reality was that I had some speed and the right mind-set for the wide receiver position. I was about five foot nine with long arms and above average hand-eye coordination. From my experience playing point guard in basketball, I had good instincts and the ability to see a play developing before it unfolded.

But I was raw. When the season started, I was still the third-string receiver.

The football team was loaded with characters. T. J. Tillman, our quarterback, was a big personality. He also had a cannon for an arm. One of our best defensive players was our starting linebacker, Chenry Lewis. Chenry was a hilarious Jamaican kid who never gave up his "Rasta" roots.

Our best player was our senior running back, a boy named Jordan Cleaves.

Jordan was our leader in every sense of the word. He was the one already taping up his ankles when you got into the locker room. "You ready to dominate today, Cruz?" he'd ask me. I was a basketball player, giving football a shot, but he always saw great potential in my skills. "You can be great, Vic," he'd tell me.

Everyone loved Jordan, and not just because of his warmth and his infectious smile. Everyone loved Jordan because of how he made you feel about yourself.

Jordan and I quickly became very close friends. He'd drive me home from football practices in his old Dodge Stratus. When petty things like playing time or an issue with a girl got me down, he'd flash a giant smile and say, "Enjoy life, Vic. We're blessed, man."

Jordan wasn't the biggest guy, but he was as strong as an ox. His best friend was a boy named Rashawn Ricks, another kid from a tough part of Paterson. Rashawn, known as "Rocky," played linebacker. Those two were inseparable, and because of them, there were always big-time college scouts at our games.

I remember in one game, Rocky went down with what appeared to be a really bad leg injury. "Hey, I'm fine," he told Coach Wimberly despite the obvious pain he was in.

He later had ten tackles and two sacks in the second half of that game. Afterward, doctors told Rocky that he had played on a partially torn anterior cruciate ligament in his knee. It was the type of injury that would end most professional players' seasons. Rocky had just laughed. "Yeah? Wow, that's crazy," he said.

He wouldn't miss a snap the remainder of the season.

COACH WIMBERLY WAS a screamer. I don't think he ever whispered anything in this life. He was always chewing and spitting out sunflower seeds. He'd be yelling something on the sideline, and at the same time this spray of sunflower seed shells would come out of his mouth. Sometimes your face would get caught in the line of fire.

Though my understanding of football was picking up, I hadn't really made much of an impact. The other starting receivers, a boy named Marcus Robinson and a tall, rangy kid named Adrian Rodriguez, knew all the routes and had a good rhythm with T.J., our quarterback. When I lined up, I'd just run as far as I could and hope T.J. would throw me a long pass. He didn't do that very often.

So I decided to change the situation.

One day after practice I knocked on Coach Wimberly's office door and asked him to teach me how to play wide receiver. He smiled. In one of the few times in his life where he didn't scream, he said, "I was wondering when this day would come, Victor."

Coach sat me down and taught me something called the "Route Tree." The Route Tree is a basic diagram that outlines all of the possible different paths a receiver can take. There were lots of different routes—Flat, Slant, Curl, Hook, Comeback, Dig, Out, Corner, Fade, Post, and Go. All season, I'd just been running Go routes, trying to run past the cornerback covering me. It was a dead sprint every single time.

Coach Wimberly drew the Route Tree on a piece of paper and told me to study it. "Once you get these routes down," he said, "you'll be a difficult guy to cover."

I studied that Route Tree like I used to study the five-page packets for The Sir. Every night, I'd quiz myself on the Five-Yard Out and the Skinny Post. My mother would sit with me at the kitchen table and show me flash cards with the routes drawn out.

I made progress. A few weeks later, Coach Wimberly lined me up at the number two wideout position. After one of our final games, Coach Wimberly handed me a glossy pamphlet. In big, bold letters, the cover read UNIVERSITY OF VIRGINIA 7-ON-7 FOOTBALL CAMP. Apparently, Al Golden, Virginia's defensive coordinator, had been in the stands scouting Rocky and he had liked the way I played.

"Coach Golden asked that I pass this along to you," Coach Wimberly told me. "He thinks you should attend their camp this summer."

Up until that moment, I had always assumed that basketball would be my ticket out of Paterson and into college. It never had crossed my mind that maybe foot-ball would take me to new and exciting places.

I signed up for that camp and spent the rest of the school year looking forward to the opportunity.

Football, huh?

Why not?

LIFE IS A TEST

ONCE THE FOOTBALL season ended, I was out of my pads and into my Nike high-tops. We had a county championship in basketball to defend.

Both Mookie and Marquis had huge years, and though Colin had moved away, we were one of the best teams in the entire state. We lost the title game to St. Patrick's, but it wasn't so bad. Mookie got a full scholarship to play center at Syracuse, and Marquis was headed to Rutgers. Jim Salmon told me that the coaches at Creighton, a Division I school in Nebraska, had asked him about me, but I wasn't sure I wanted to play basketball in college anymore.

ON A SATURDAY morning in June of my junior year, I popped my head into Teddy's bodega and grabbed a banana and a Capri Sun juice box out of the refrigerator in the back.

"What's up, Vic?" Teddy asked. "Why are you up so early on a Saturday morning?"

"I'm taking the SATs today, Teddy. They say I need a banana and some vitamin C."

When I got to the testing center in a nearby high

school, I looked around the class and saw a bunch of strange faces. For whatever reason, I couldn't focus. I had always been good at English class, but those analogies on the SATs just didn't make much sense. Math wasn't my best subject, but I had trouble answering even the easiest questions. By the time I reached the final section, I had completely spaced out.

I finished the test and didn't think twice about it. I was just happy to be done.

I got my score in the mail a few weeks later. A 720.

You get two hundred points just for filling in your name.

I wasn't overly concerned with my performance, but my mother was alarmed. "Victor, you can't get into any good colleges with a 720," she said. I didn't want to hear it. I knew I could take the test again in the fall.

Coach Wimberly was a bit concerned about the score too. He called me in to his office and explained that I'd never play college football if I couldn't get high enough SAT scores to qualify academically.

It didn't make sense to me. But it was true whether I liked it or not.

THE UNIVERSITY OF Virginia football camp was the first week I had ever spent away from my friends, family, Jim, and everyone else I knew. I had been to some cool places and seen some really great things, but I had never really been on my own.

At UVA they paired us off into groups of two and put us in dorm rooms. The player everyone noticed at once was a guy from Louisiana named Early Doucet. He looked like a grown man at the age of seventeen. He was six feet tall, weighed two hundred pounds, and ran like the wind.

I'd never seen a wide receiver like him before.

When we got on the field that first morning, I lined up at cornerback against him. As the play unfolded, a pass was thrown above my head, and I figured it was headed out of bounds. With one hand, Early reached out over my shoulder and hauled it in.

He then went eighty yards for a touchdown.

I got burned a few dozen times that week, but I made a few good plays myself. The last night, one of the assistant coaches knocked on my dorm room door and told me that everyone was thrilled with the way I had played.

I left camp feeling good about my performance and my chances at becoming a college football player. Of course, I also wondered how I'd ever make it to the NFL with specimens like Early Doucet roaming the planet.

THERE WAS A ton of buzz surrounding our football team heading into my senior year. We had some great younger guys on the team who were ready to take their games to the next level. Kit Pommels was our Devin Hester. He'd return kicks, play running back, and fill the second receiver role. Our new starting running back, a junior named Tymier Wells, was a worthy replacement for Jordan. He ran the ball hard, and he never fumbled. Both the *Newark Star-Ledger* and the *Bergen Record* ran newspaper articles about our team. Every major New Jersey news outlet predicted us to win the state championship.

When we got to practice that August, Coach Wimberly introduced a new play to the offense: Twins Right Tarzan.

I loved Twins Right Tarzan.

The play lined both Kit and me to the right of our quarterback, T.J. When the ball was snapped, we'd both run ten yards and crisscross. Kit would make a cut toward the middle of the field and I'd go deep on a post pattern.

We must have run Twins Right Tarzan ten times a game, and it worked just about every time.

That 2003 season was just plain silly. We blew all of our opponents out, and everyone put up huge individual statistics. In half of our games, we'd be so far ahead at halftime that T.J., Kit, and I would sit out the third and fourth quarters.

One game against Elmwood Park was supposed to be very competitive. They'd had a few big wins early in the season and there were articles suggesting they'd give us a good fight.

I ended up scoring five touchdowns in the first two quarters in five different ways: a kick return, an interception return, a punt return, a rushing touchdown on a reverse play, and a receiving touchdown on Twins Right Tarzan. There was a kid at St. Mary High School that season scoring eight and nine touchdowns a game. Having had five in the first half, I wanted to score ten or eleven. But Coach Wimberly kept me on the sidelines. "We don't do that at Paterson Catholic," he told me. "We always win with class."

I had over eight hundred receiving yards and caught nineteen touchdown passes my senior year.

But the college scouts weren't impressed.

I'd ask Coach Wimberly why none of the big schools were interested in me. He didn't know. He was as confused as I was. "You'll get your shot, Victor," he'd say. "I'm not sure where, but you'll get your shot. And you'll prove them all wrong."

I played most of that season with a giant chip on my shoulder. I was constantly trying to prove myself to those scouts. I wanted to show them that I, Victor Cruz, was the playmaker they needed on their teams in the Big East or the SEC.

But ten games came and ten games went and no Division I-A schools came calling. College coaches would tell Coach Wimberly that, at five foot nine, I was just too small to play wide receiver for a big-time college football program.

I spent endless hours on recruiting Web sites reading about guys like Ted Ginn Jr., a five-star recruit from Cleveland, Ohio, and Adrian Peterson, a big running back from Palestine, Texas. I wondered if I'd ever get the chance to line up against them. Maybe they were bigger, stronger, and faster than I was, but I knew nobody wanted it more than me.

We went undefeated during the regular season, setting up a state championship game against Bayley-Ellard High School.

MAYBE THEY WERE BIGGER, STRONGER, AND FASTER THAN I WAS, BUT I KNEW NOBODY WANTED IT MORE THAN ME.

Everyone in Paterson attended that game. There were grown men watching on the roofs of their cars with little kids sitting on their shoulders. We came out strong and had our best effort of the season, beating them with ease. After the game, I posed for a photograph with my parents that I still have in a frame right by my bed.

Though I had my heart set on playing for a major Division I-A college program, Coach Wimberly suggested that I meet with a few of the Division I-AA coaches who were asking about me. I initially resisted the idea because Division I-AA was a step down on the ladder. But then I spoke with my old teammate Jordan Cleaves. He too had been a star at the high school level. And no Division I-A teams had recruited him either.

He had ended up going to Virginia State University, a Division II school, which was another step down from I-AA. I called him up on the phone to discuss my future. "Victor, you don't need to be a small fish in a big pond," he said. "You're better than that. If you were to go to Rutgers or West Virginia, you'd just be another guy from New Jersey fighting for playing time. Go visit those Division I-AA schools and become a star."

After a pause, he added, "We'll be teammates in the NFL someday, man. We'll buy our mothers mansions and wear Super Bowl rings around Paterson. Go to a smaller school and prove everyone wrong."

Jordan Cleaves always had the right thing to say. He may have been slightly crazy with all of his talk about the NFL and mansions for our mothers, but he was a believer. He saw something special in me when a lot of others didn't.

So my mother and I visited Hofstra University, a Division I-AA school up in Long Island. Two juniors on the team gave me a tour of the school, and the coach, Joe Gardi, told me they'd be thrilled to have me on their squad.

I also visited the University of Delaware. Though I didn't end up joining the Fighting Blue Hens football team, I sometimes wonder what it would have been like if I had. A year after my recruiting trip there, a quarterback from South Jersey named Joe Flacco transferred there from the University of Pittsburgh, where he'd lost the starting job.

I was sold on the University of Massachusetts Amherst the second I stepped foot on campus. Located in a woodsy town about ninety miles west of Boston, it reminded me of the beautiful green campuses in Durham and Charlottesville. The football team's head coach, a guy named Mark Whipple, said that they'd had their eyes on me all season.

On my official visit, I got to hang out with some of the older guys on the squad. We hit it off right away. Shannon James, the team's top defensive back, and James Ihedigbo, a starting safety from western Massachusetts, told me about their recruiting experiences. Our stories were all so similar. They too had experienced outstanding high school football careers. But the big-time Division I-A programs never came knocking. "So we came here," Ihedigbo told me. "And guess what? We got playing time right away and we love it. I'd probably still be stuck on the bench if I was playing somewhere else."

My mother loved UMass too, and Coach Whipple told me, "Victor, a full scholarship is yours. You just need to get those SAT scores up."

I gave my verbal commitment to Coach Whipple and went back to Paterson with a Minutemen Football sweatshirt that I wore everywhere around town. I was going to college and I was going to play football.

I just needed to conquer the SATs.

AS MY SENIOR season on the basketball team began, my mind wasn't focused on pick-and-rolls and offensive rebounds. All I could think about were my SAT scores.

I took the test, again, in December and got an 840. It still was not a high enough score to play football at the next level.

In January of my senior year, I got a text message that read "You around?"

I called back, and reached Shannon James. "Hey, Victor. I didn't want you to hear this from someone else first. Coach Whipple just announced that he's leaving us to become the quarterbacks coach of the Pittsburgh Steelers."

I panicked. Who was the new coach going to be? Would he know my name? Would I fit into his offensive system? More importantly, did I still have my scholarship?

A few days later, I heard from the new coach, a man named Don Brown. When I spoke with Coach Brown, he said that his staff was very excited about having a guy like me joining the program. At the end of the phone call, though, he said something along the lines of "Now, just go ace those SATs."

The basketball season went well. We played some of the best teams in the country and did more than hold our own. The whole season built up toward a big game versus St. Patrick's, a rival Catholic school from a few towns over. St. Pat's had always been good, but that season they were fantastic.

It was going to be a televised game, and all of Paterson was abuzz. One day during practice that week, someone special paid us a visit.

Right through the gym doors, dressed in more bling than you'd find in Tiffany, came Tim Thomas.

"Coach Patterson, can I talk to these kids?" he asked.

Thomas, the hero of so many of our childhoods, brought us into a tight huddle.

"I've been following you guys all season," he said. He then pointed to each of our team's starting five. One by one, he told us about what we were each doing right and wrong. Tim Thomas was averaging thirty-two minutes a night and scoring fourteen points per game in the NBA, but he had taken the time to check out the Paterson Catholic basketball team.

"Paterson's a part of me," he said. "It always has been and it always will be. Someday you will all understand. Always be proud of being from Paterson. Always."

Paterson wasn't just some town in New Jersey. Paterson was more. It molded boys into men. We went out and won the game versus St. Patrick's, and Tim Thomas cheered from the stands.

I took the SATs a third time in February. Back then, you could dial an 800 number and get your scores over the phone instead of waiting the extra few days to get them in the mail. When the automated voice revealed my score, my heart sank. An 820, even lower than the last time I'd taken it.

But I wasn't done yet. After the basketball season ended, I prepared long and hard, taking out every SAT prep book in the school library and doing practice exams at home. My mother would serve as the proctor and sit with an egg timer as I ripped through the sections. I did well on those practice tests and built up my confidence.

But on the day of the April exam, my head was just

somewhere else. I couldn't focus. I blamed the weather outside. I blamed the pressure.

When I got the score of that fourth attempt back in the mail, I was beside myself. An 820. Again.

0 for 4.

I got on the phone with the UMass admissions office. A woman there told me I had to get at least a 920 to qualify for the 2004 college football campaign. I'd have one more chance to take the test in June.

So I hit the books. Hard. The test prep books, my old trigonometry books from my sophomore year, my thesaurus—I had them all in a stack on the nightstand by my bed. I stopped playing video games and going to the park for basketball after school. I didn't spend late nights on the phone with the girls Pelli and I had met at Skaters World.

I was an SAT studying machine.

I took the test on another sunny morning in June. When I was done, I had a good feeling leaving the room. I hadn't zoned out, I had finished all five sections, and I hadn't left many questions blank.

No one had ever gone to college on the Cruz side of my family. My mother, my *abuela*, and *Papí* took so much pride in telling everyone back in Puerto Rico that I was going to the University of Massachusetts Amherst in the fall. Nothing made them happier than the fact that I was college-bound.

When the envelope came in the mail a month later, I stared at it for an hour before opening it up.

Then, like quickly ripping off a Band-Aid, I dove into the envelope to find out my score.

900.

I'd fallen twenty points short.

My father came over to the house that night. He said I shouldn't let the news defeat me. When my mother and I spoke with Coach Brown and the folks in the UMass admissions office, they explained that my scholarship wasn't being pulled. It'd just be put on hold until I got the necessary SAT scores.

"So, when's the next test?" my mother asked, thinking the answer would be July or August.

"October," the admissions woman responded.

October? That was still five months away.

"What am I supposed to do until then?" I asked. Wasn't there some way I could at least come to campus with the other freshmen for orientation in August?

It was Coach Brown who explained the next step he had in mind. For the upcoming fall semester, I'd go to something called a "prep school." There I'd take a few courses, play football, and focus on raising my SAT scores.

It sounded like prison. And the worst part? The school he had in mind was in Maine, eight hours away from home.

It was a lot to digest at once, but Coach Brown said that this was a common path to college for young men in my position.

I had no other choice. I was headed to Maine.

IF YOU WERE a teenager in northern New Jersey during the 1990s and 2000s, you built your summers around the July Fourth fair at the Meadowlands. Each year around Independence Day, they'd turn the parking lot in between Giants Stadium and the IZOD Center into a giant carnival with rides, games, and concession stands. The fair was like the dance floor at Skaters World times a million.

I was so upset about my SATs that I didn't really enjoy senior week or my high school graduation. I moped around everywhere with a "Woe Is Me" grimace on my face. It took until the July Fourth fair for me to come out of my funk.

Jordan and Rocky were both back from college, and I was excited to see them. Jordan had heard all about my situation, and he told me to quit pitying myself. "We're blessed, Vic," he said. "Don't stress out, man. Someday, when we're both in the NFL, we'll laugh about this."

He was right. So I'd have to wait a semester before I got to college. Big deal. Unlike most of the kids I grew up with, I still had that opportunity. I had a great group of friends, a mother and father who loved me, and a bright future ahead.

After the fireworks display and about three cotton candies too many, I gave Jordan a hug and told him I'd call him the next day. It had been great seeing him.

I caught up with some of the kids in my grade, and we hung out at the fair well past midnight. We were all going our separate ways in the fall—some to college, some to the military, some back to Paterson, and one to a prep school in Bridgton, Maine.

On the car ride back home from the Meadowlands, my friend Julissa got a phone call. As she answered it, she leaned forward and turned down the radio.

"What?!" she asked in a horrified tone.

Then she started sobbing uncontrollably.

"What is it?" I asked, knowing something bad must have happened.

She couldn't breathe. She started screaming, "No! No!"

We pulled the car over, and I took her outside.

"Julissa, what is it? What happened?" I feared the absolute worst.

Through her tears, she looked straight at me. "Jordan Cleaves died in a car accident tonight."

That wasn't possible. I'd been with Jordan the entire day. I had just said good-bye to him a few hours earlier. I told her she was wrong.

"Vic, he's dead. Jordan's dead," she said. "He was driving home in the rain, and his car flipped over on Route Twenty."

I couldn't feel my knees. I fell to the ground and immediately started crying.

As Julissa got more details on the accident, the news only got worse. Jordan wasn't driving home alone that night. Rocky, Rocky's brother Marquette, and Marquette's friend Donald were all in the car too.

Jordan, Marquette, and Donald had all died instantly from the sudden impact of the crash. Rocky was in critical condition at the hospital.

"They don't think Rocky's going to make it," she said. "And if he does, he'll never walk again."

Rocky was a 240-pound tackling machine. I had seen him record ten tackles on a torn ACL. Now he was never going to walk again?

I attended Jordan's wake and funeral, but none of it felt real. To this day, I still get the urge to pick up the phone and call him.

Rocky, however, survived the crash. When he woke up from the accident a few days later, he didn't remember a thing. He couldn't move his neck, though. The doctors told him he'd be fortunate to walk again.

Not only did Rashawn "Rocky" Ricks walk again, but he was back on his feet and training for football season a few months later. He never did play, though, because the medical professionals all said he'd risk paralysis if he took a bad hit to the neck.

Rocky could have let the news crush him and ruin his spirit. But he was a fighter.

For the next four years, Rocky was a student assistant on the Rutgers football team, serving as a part-time coach for the defensive ends and linebackers. He lugged equipment to practices, watched game tape late into the evening hours, and scouted all the opposing teams. He never made another tackle, but he still made a tremendous impact. Rashawn Ricks graduated from Rutgers in four years and still checks in on me today.

AS I WAS getting mentally prepared for my departure to prep school, Pelli called me up in late August. He was seeing a girl named Tara from Passaic, and she had some friends he thought I should meet.

"Tara's friends are hot, man," he said. "And you're not going to be seeing any women for the next few months. It might be good to talk to some girls while you can."

I felt like a sailor being sent out to sea.

In theory, his idea was great, except for the fact that we were seventeen and we were meeting these girls at The Wild Bull, a twenty-one-and-over bar in Clifton.

We didn't have fake IDs, we weren't big drinkers, and we certainly didn't look twenty-one years old. Fortunately, we were with Pelli's girl, and underage girls get to play by different rules when it comes to getting into bars.

Pelli's girl was cute and friendly, but her friends hadn't arrived yet. As we waited, Pelli and I posted up at the bar, trying to fit in. After a few hours of waiting, I got restless. I told Pelli I was going to head home.

"You've got to stay, man. Stay for me."

If seventeen-year-old Victor Cruz was anything, he was a good wingman.

When her friends finally arrived, one stood out from the pack. She was an absolute knockout.

I was always pretty smooth with the opposite sex—or at least I thought I was—but when I saw this girl, I was tongue-tied.

She strutted over to our table like she owned the place.

The way every guy was staring at her, she damn well could have owned it.

"I'm Elaina." She smiled, extending her hand in my direction.

"Uh, I'm Vic," I said.

Barely.

We made small talk for a few minutes before going our separate ways. I left The Wild Bull that night thinking I might have been drunk. I also left *knowing* that I was in love.

The next morning, I woke up at seven and called Pelli. He wasn't used to early-morning phone calls. "What's wrong, dude?" he asked, still half asleep.

"When are we hanging out with those girls again?"

Pelli laughed. "You think you've got a chance with Elaina, don't you?"

It turned out that Elaina was more than just a pretty face. She had graduated from high school at the age of fifteen. Here I was just getting ready to attend prep school, and she was heading into her junior year at Florida International University.

A few nights later, we snuck into another twenty-one-and-over bar. When Elaina walked in, she took my breath away. Again.

Instead of staring at her from a distance, drooling like a dog, I decided to play it somewhat cooler. There were other girls in the club, so I started dancing with them. Every so often, I'd look in her direction and catch her glancing back at me.

As I was talking with one of the other girls, someone bumped me hard in the back. I turned around, thinking it was a drunk guy losing control.

It was Elaina.

"Oh, I'm sorry. I didn't see you there." She smiled.

It was no accident.

Trying to be cool, I backed away and walked to the other end of the bar. She shrugged and started dancing with another guy.

Had I blown it? Was she going to end up with the other

dude for the rest of the night? I called Pelli over to discuss it.

"Just play it cool," he said. "And stop running away from her."

A few minutes later, Elaina left the dance floor and walked right over to me. "What's up with you?" she asked. "Are you shy or something?"

"I'm not shy." I smiled back. "I'm not shy at all."

From that moment on, we were inseparable. We started dating almost immediately and realized we had a lot in common. Like me, Elaina was half black and half Puerto Rican. She too had big dreams, and had started on the path to achieving them. We introduced each other to our families and spoke all day and night on the phone.

"That girl's going to be the mother of my baby someday," I told my mom.

I wasn't kidding.

THE REAL WORLD

THE DRIVE UP to Bridgton was straight out of a bad movie. My mother and father were in the front seats of my mom's Ford Explorer. I was in the back. Every thirty minutes, I'd ask, "Are we there yet?"

The answer was always "Not even close."

For a kid from Paterson, Bridgton was no different than the planet Mars. It was way up in the woods of Maine. But I wasn't at Bridgton Academy to make friends or explore the wonders of the Pine Tree State. I was there to raise my SAT scores.

My days at Bridgton were focused on two things: the SATs and Elaina. She and I would write cheesy love letters and e-mails, encouraging each other to chase our dreams.

I was madly in love.

The week before I took the SATs in October, I had a long talk with my mother on the telephone. She told me to just relax and walk into the room with a clear head.

"Everyone's so proud of you, regardless of the score you get on your SATs, Victor."

I was now confident I could do well enough to move

on to the next phase of my life. I entered the testing center without a banana or a juice box.

Four weeks later, I got my score in the mail.

A 1040.

I had knocked it out of the park. I called everyone I knew, starting with Elaina. She was thrilled.

I'D BE THE FIRST CRUZ TO GO TO COLLEGE.

My mother, *abuela*, and *Papí* were all overjoyed. I'd be the first Cruz to go to college.

My father was excited too. He asked me when the first game of the following college football season would be. "I'll be there," he assured me, "screaming from the stands."

I GOT TO UMass in the spring of 2005 and was blown away.

Everyone was nice. Everyone was cool. Everyone was beautiful. Girls I'd never met before were waving to me across the Student Union. Dudes I didn't know were offering to help carry my bags.

The older guys on the team, who had taken me around campus fourteen months earlier, were all excited about my arrival. They initiated me into their group the only way they knew how.

We partied.

And we partied hard.

I'd worked so much just to get into college that once I finally got there, I wanted to celebrate. I forgot all about studying, schoolwork, or even attending class. Who cared about any of that? I was a big-time college football player now.

My roommate freshman year was a great kid named Shawnn Gyles. Shawnn was a safety on the team, which made our pairing as roommates awfully interesting on the football field. We got up at five thirty in the morning every day that spring, sleepwalking together to practices. Then we went at it one-on-one for three hours straight. The moment practice ended and the final whistle blew, we'd leave it on the field and return to being the best of friends.

When I finished that first semester, I might have been the coolest guy on campus. But my grade point average was an appalling 1.6.

The dean of admissions called me into her office and told me that I'd need to raise my overall GPA above a 2.0 not only to stay on the football team, but to remain at UMass.

I said I understood and headed home to Paterson.

School was out for summer.

SHAWNN DIDN'T RETURN to UMass that fall, and I was excited to meet my new roommate.

Liam Coen was a six-foot-two skinny white kid with strawberry blond hair from a small town in Rhode Island. He was also a hell of a quarterback. Liam didn't have the strongest arm, but he was an incredibly accurate passer. Liam could hit any receiver, in any situation, right in the numbers on the front of his jersey.

I was redshirted that year, meaning I'd watch the 2005 games from the sidelines. It wasn't a punishment. Instead of throwing me to the wolves before I was ready, Coach Brown felt that a year of observing and learning would do me some good. Except for the really rare talents that play right away, most college football players are redshirted for their first season.

Though I couldn't suit up for games, I could still practice. I was on the scout team, which meant that I had to learn the upcoming opposing team's offense and play the position of their number one receiver against our starting defense each week in practice. Scout team guys aren't supposed to give the starters trouble, but I was giving our top cornerbacks and safeties lots of headaches.

"Cruz, we're lucky we don't have to play against you on Saturdays," James Ihedigbo, our top safety, would tell me after practices.

"You're still raw, Victor, but you could end up being one of our starting receivers next year," Coach Brown told me one day after a particularly strong practice. "Just keep up the hard work. And get your academics in order, son."

Unlike Paterson Catholic, where the classes were small and the teachers knew the students by their first names, the UMass lecture halls were massive. The introductory courses that I was taking that year had fifteen hundred students in them.

I found excuses for everything. When I'd get an F on an assignment, I wouldn't let it bother me. I'd rationalize things. "Why should I spend time learning about the War of 1812 if I am torching Shannon James in practice every day?"

I didn't attend many classes, and when I did, I'd usually just put my head down on my desk and take a nap.

My behavior was shameful.

On exam days, I'd show up and just assume I'd copy off someone else in the class. If the other students didn't *let* me cheat off them, I'd get angry. "Goody Two-shoes," I'd mutter, and they'd roll their eyes.

I had been blessed with the opportunity of a lifetime— a full-time college scholarship—and was too busy with video games and late nights at The Pub to realize that it was slipping all away. The success was getting to my head. In truth, it wasn't even any actual success at all. I wasn't even playing on Saturdays; I was just on the scout team. I was an above average *practice* player.

When my mother called, she'd ask about my grades,

and I'd blatantly lie to her. I'd say they were fine.

Elaina and I were also growing more and more distant. Days would go by where I wouldn't hear from her, and I'd barely notice. I was too busy having fun with the other guys. I'd go out until all hours of the night and wake up at noon.

My inflated ego had gotten out of control. And without having Elaina, my mother, my father, Coach Wimberly, Jim Salmon, or Jordan Cleaves around to bring me back down to Earth, I lost sight of my goals.

I went home for the holidays thinking all was good in the world of Victor Cruz. When my grades arrived in an e-mail a few days before Christmas, the reality of the situation became clear.

My GPA was a 1.8 for the semester, and a 1.7 overall. Anything less than a 2.0 average wouldn't cut it.

I was expelled.

I hadn't played in a single football game, and I was already kicked out of college.

I figured there had to be some kind of mistake. There was no way they could just boot me out of UMass. Not when I was playing so well in those practices. Not when everyone on campus was telling me how great I was. Not when I hadn't paid for a drink at The Pub all semester.

But it was the truth.

■ ■ ■ ■

ELAINA CAME OVER that night to help me write a letter to the dean of admissions while I broke the news to my mother. The former was a lot easier than the latter.

My mother was so proud of the fact that her son was in college. She had told everyone she knew. She wore her UMass shirts and hats everywhere she went in town. She loved that I had worked so hard to get there.

In less than eight months, I'd squandered it all away.

When I showed her my grades and explained what they meant, she didn't say a word. She just shook her head in disappointment. My mother always had an answer for everything. An old saying, a joke, a quip—something.

The news of my expulsion left her speechless.

I sent a detailed e-mail to the admissions office asking what I could do to get back into school. The response wasn't exactly what I had hoped.

No matter what, I'd have to miss the spring 2006 semester at UMass.

I could enroll in classes at a local community college, but there was no guarantee that I'd be readmitted after that. I called Coach Brown, but he told me there was really nothing he could do.

A few days after the New Year's holiday, I drove my mother's car to the County College of Morris. I walked in and signed up for a full slate of courses. I was back at stage one.

AS A YOUNG boy in our apartment on East Twentieth Street, I'd marvel at how *Papí* lived his life according to a strict schedule. He was a creature of habit.

Those next six months I was too. Every weekday, I'd wake up at seven a.m. and drive my mother to her job at Benjamin Moore Paints. After dropping her off, I'd take the car to school and stay until six p.m. At six thirty, I'd pick her up from work and drive us home. We'd have dinner and I'd go to bed.

Rinse and repeat.

Occasionally, I'd drive down Park Avenue and see guys I grew up with, wearing new clothes and hanging out. They always seemed to be having so much fun, and girls were always buzzing around them like bees on honey.

It would have been easy to blow off a class here or there and join them, but I resisted. My goal was to get back into UMass, and nothing was going to get in my way.

At the end of May, I sent my County College of Morris, spring 2006 semester transcript to the admissions office at UMass. Three B's and an A.

In early June, I got a formal letter back in the mail. It started with "Congratulations!"

Though my grades didn't transfer over to my grade point average, I could return to campus and the team in the fall.

I was excited to get back to school that August. I called up Liam to see if he'd be my roommate in the dorms. I couldn't imagine living with anyone else.

"I've got the *Madden* game cued up and ready to go," he laughed.

I was happy to be back on the squad. Whereas Liam was now our starting quarterback, Coach Brown still didn't think I was ready for playing time on the field.

I was disappointed, but I understood Coach Brown's decision. The offense was running a complex offensive scheme, and I had missed months of practice in the spring. There was just no way he could put me into a game.

"Use this season to watch how the older guys go about their business," he told me.

I felt that I was one of the best athletes on the team. But being the best athlete doesn't necessarily make you the best player. The game of football is one of physical skills, but it's also quite cerebral. I didn't get on the field once during that 2006 season.

■ ■ ■ ■

I *THOUGHT* I'D done significantly better in school that fall, but when my grades came in an e-mail that December, the news was bleak.

I'd gotten a 2.2 for the semester, which was better than before, but not better enough. My cumulative grade point average was still below a 2.0.

So I got kicked out of school. Again.

I called Coach Brown, but he'd had more than enough conversations with me about my grades. "You're like a broken record, Victor," he said. "I don't know what to tell you this time. How many strikes do you want? How many strikes do you expect?"

My mother and I hopped in her Ford Explorer and drove four hours to Amherst. We arrived at the office of Pamela Marsh-Williams, the associate dean for undergraduate advising. She'd never seen or heard of me before.

"Victor, I'll be honest, your options are quite limited," she told me as she thumbed through my transcript.

My mother was distraught. She explained to Ms. Marsh-Williams what I'd been through, what I'd overcome to make it to UMass.

But Ms. Marsh-Williams didn't budge. "I'm impressed with Victor's story, Ms. Cruz," she said. "But once he got here, he *stopped* working."

As it turned out, not only did I have awful grades, I wasn't even enrolled in the right classes. There were several key core classes that I still hadn't taken.

"You have to go back home to Paterson and find an accredited institution," she explained. "When you do, you're going to have to take several classes—more than you've ever taken in a semester here—and earn very high marks in all of them."

I was scribbling notes in a spiral notebook, nodding, and not saying a word. Though she didn't have to, Ms. Marsh-Williams went online and identified some of the different community colleges in northern New Jersey where my credits *and* grades would transfer.

"You're no longer a student here, Victor," she told me as we wrapped up the conversation. "I can't do much more for you. It's on you now."

My scholarship was revoked, and I removed all of my belongings from the dorm. I climbed into my mother's car with my tail between my legs.

We didn't speak the entire four-hour drive home.

MOM HAD PAID for my high school education at Paterson Catholic and taken out a loan for my semester in Bridgton. It wasn't right to ask her to pay the tuition at Passaic County Community College. I'd have to get a job.

I put on a nice pair of slacks and a button-down shirt.

Then I went to the Garden State Plaza, an upscale shopping mall in Paramus.

I'd always liked men's fashion. I figured if I was going to work in a mall smelling the Cinnabon store all day, I might as well get a decent employee discount out of it. I walked into the GUESS store, visualizing myself as a suave salesman selling designer jeans.

"What's your story?" the manager, an attractive woman in her late twenties, asked me.

I told her that I was home from college and needed some extra cash. I'd work hard and show up every day with a smile.

"So, sell me some jeans," she responded.

"What?"

"What do you mean 'What?' If I were a customer walking into this store today, what would your sales pitch be? Sell me some GUESS jeans."

I was caught off guard. I'd never *sold* anything before. I certainly hadn't sold $120 designer jeans.

"Hey, I'm Victor," I started.

"Are you trying to pick me up?" she snapped back. "I'm here to buy jeans. I don't care what your name is."

"Yeah, so, uh, what style are you looking for, ma'am?" I mumbled.

"What style am I looking for? You're the salesman. Should I go online and come back and tell you what style

I'm looking for? Or should I just go to another store where they'll tell me what style looks best on me?"

I shook the woman's hand and thanked her for her time.

A bit discouraged, I stumbled into a men's clothing store called Image. The manager was a young guy named Jeff. I told him I was interested in working there and that I liked the lines they carried.

Jeff looked at me and nodded. "Can you start tomorrow?" he asked.

"I can start today," I answered.

Jeff hired me on the spot. I alternated every day between going to classes and working eight-hour shifts at Image.

My shifts at the mall were long and tedious. There were no chairs at Image, so I was always on my feet. Jeff gave his employees a thirty-minute lunch break, but by the time I'd get to the food court across the mall, fifteen of those thirty minutes were already gone. I remember sneaking into the men's restroom on the second floor and locking myself behind a toilet stall door. I wouldn't use the facilities. I'd just sit. It felt so good to just sit.

One day that January, I was unloading boxes in the back room when I heard a commotion coming from the front of the store. I popped my head out to see what was going on.

Michael Strahan, a defensive end on the Giants, had

walked into Image and a mob of fans had followed him. I watched as Strahan posed for photographs. With his smile and humility, he made every one of those fans feel like the most important person in the store.

I kept my distance until Jeff called to me. "Vic, you've got to meet Michael Strahan."

I put the box cutter down and shuffled over to greet the Giants All-Pro.

"Vic's a football player," Jeff told Strahan, putting his arm around my shoulder. "He played wide receiver at UMass. He's back home getting his grades in order. This kid's a tremendously hard worker."

Strahan smiled and told me to keep on working hard. "I went to Texas Southern," he said. "Texas Southern, man. The NFL will find you if you're good enough."

Strahan bought a pair of jeans, signed a few autographs, and was on his way. But his message that day was clear. For all the ups and downs I'd been through, I was still just twenty years old.

If the NFL could find Michael Strahan at tiny Texas Southern, they could certainly find me at UMass.

I just needed to get back there.

WHILE I WAS busy with courses and spending long hours on my feet at the mall, things weren't going very well for other members of my family.

Papí was sick.

"Your grandfather has colon cancer," my mother told me one day when I was studying at the kitchen table.

Week after week, I'd visit *Papí* and see a shell of the guy I once wrestled with as a kid. As the cancer spread, he aged considerably and lost a lot of weight.

My father was in a dark place too.

In February of that year, I got a call from my older sister, Ebony. She had recently given birth to a beautiful baby boy and I was thrilled to be an uncle. Jordan Turner was Dad's first grandchild.

Now, though, Ebony was fed up. She and my father had been fighting a lot. In their most recent phone call, he had cursed her out and called her several nasty names.

Ebony had always been the apple of my father's eye. She was crushed by his harsh words.

I couldn't understand how he could speak to his only daughter that way. She was a young, single mother and she needed the emotional support of her father. I was disgusted by his behavior and I called him to let him know.

We went at it. I said some mean things that I probably shouldn't have, and he did the same. He was already mad at me for getting kicked out of school. My phone call only enraged him more.

Before hanging up, I told him that I never wanted to speak to him again.

■ ■ ■ ■

MAYBE I COULD have been more understanding.

My father worked twenty-five years for the Paterson Fire Department. In the winter of 2006, he had gotten in a serious car accident. When he visited a doctor after the crash, he was told that he'd have to take some time away from work.

My father had never used a sick day in all the years he fought fires. I don't recall him ever taking a vacation either. Dad hated missing a day of work.

Following the doctor's orders, he begrudgingly went on disability leave. Dad was in chronic pain from the injury, but he was still a few years away from receiving his pension. He couldn't risk losing his job before he hit that benchmark. When he spoke with his fire chief about coming back to work, he asked to be put on light duty, which was common for a firefighter returning to work after a bad accident.

His request was denied.

He returned to work far sooner than he should have. Still, he was getting back into his normal routine when he began feeling sharp pains in his stomach and chest. Vomiting and nausea soon followed. He went back to the doctor and soon learned that he had liver disease.

He hit a new low in March. After twenty-five years on

the job, and just a few months after surviving the accident, he was fired.

There'd been a long history of racial tension within the Paterson Fire Department. In 2004, a group of Paterson's African-American and Latino firefighters had filed a civil complaint, alleging racial discrimination in the department's hiring practices. The case was settled when both groups agreed to implement a new program committed to bringing in qualified minority candidates.

In May of 2006, my father and four other African-American firefighters in Paterson filed another lawsuit against the fire department. They alleged discrimination, harassment, and unruly retaliation from their supervisors. My father didn't think he had been fired because of his performance, his illness, or a head-count issue. He believed it was because he had spoken out against his bosses during that 2004 trial.

As he awaited a ruling and his reinstatement to the department, his medical coverage ran out.

Like *Papí*, he began to rapidly lose weight. He stopped seeing his doctor.

He was angry, he was hurt, and he was very ill.

His personality changed over the course of those months. I was upset with how he had spoken to Ebony and the things he had said to me. Sure, he was going through some rough times, but we all were.

I loved my father so much. I thought that if I gave him the silent treatment for a few months, he'd snap out of his funk.

That change never came.

ON MARCH 1, 2007, I was sitting at my computer when my older brother Malik's phone number flashed on my cell phone. We'd text each other all the time, but Malik and I rarely spoke on the phone. I answered with a bit of apprehension.

"It's Daddy, Vic," he said with a trembling voice. "They found Daddy, Vic. He's dead."

I told him to shut up and I hung up the phone.

He immediately called me back. "I don't have time for this, Malik," I told him, not wanting to even acknowledge what he had said.

"Vic, he's dead. Daddy's dead."

I went silent.

I couldn't react. I didn't know *how* to react. I felt numb.

My mother then called me from her office at work. "Your father's gone, Victor," she cried. "I'm so sorry."

I didn't truly believe he was gone until I saw his face in the open casket at his wake a few days later. At least four hundred people came to pay their respects at the New AME Zion Church.

I didn't cry at the wake or the funeral. Everyone was

hysterical around me, but I didn't shed a tear. I couldn't. I didn't think he'd want me to show emotion. He would have said, "Be strong, Vic. Be strong."

Elaina and I hadn't spoken for months, but she made the trip to Paterson for my father's funeral. We stayed up late, just talking, and we worked through some of the anger and sadness I had bottled up inside.

ONE NIGHT THAT April, I went out with a group of the Paterson guys to see Cancun, an aspiring rapper we knew, perform. It felt good to blow off some steam. I'd done nothing but study, work, and mourn over the past several weeks. I had a few drinks, a ton of laughs, and even hit the dance floor. Just as Cancun took the stage, though, a brawl between two rival gangs broke out in the middle of the club.

The last thing I needed was to be a part of a stupid fight. I headed for the exit. As I bobbed and weaved my way through the frantic crowd, I heard the sound of gunshots.

Wap-wap-wap!

It was the same noise I'd heard all those nights in my bedroom on East Eighteenth Street. Everyone in the club screamed, scattered, and ran for cover under tables and chairs.

I just kept walking.

When I got outside, I caught my breath and sat on the curb. I stared at the sky and took a deep breath.

At that moment, something clicked.

I decided that I was going to ace my final exams, get back into school, and achieve all of my goals.

No more excuses. No more pitying myself. No more sleepless nights staring at the ceiling wondering how I had pissed it all away.

My friends came running out of the club a few minutes later. They were all fired up. Someone had pushed someone, someone's girlfriend was shoved in the back, and someone said something about another guy's cousin. I loved all those guys, but I didn't care.

"I'm sorry, guys. I'm done. I'm going home."

I knew what I had to do.

CHAPTER 7

COURTESY OF LIAM COEN

WAITING FOR A CHANCE

NEWLY ENERGIZED TO hit the books, I approached the next few months at PCCC like I would a big football game. I circled the dates of my final exams and created detailed work-back plans.

Meanwhile, though I tried to convince myself that I didn't care how others viewed my situation, I hated the whispers. Everywhere I went in town, I'd catch people pointing and talking to their friends. They saw me as another Paterson failure, another local kid given a golden ticket for a better life who had thrown it all away.

I took five courses at PCCC that semester, and each one of them fulfilled a core curriculum requirement at UMass. By the time I sat down to take my exams in May, I knew all five subjects inside and out.

When I got my grades back later that month, I smiled for the first time in what felt like an eternity.

Five courses—four A's and one B. All the grades were transferable to the University of Massachusetts Amherst.

I called the admissions office. If I could get the paperwork over in a few days, I'd be a candidate for readmission into school.

In early June, I got the word. I was accepted.

It was the fourth time in three years that I celebrated getting into UMass.

INSTEAD OF HANGING around Paterson the rest of the summer, I decided to leave for school and get a head start on things. I knew a bunch of the football guys were renting an off-campus house and wondered if they'd mind adding one more roommate.

I just happened to know the right guy to call.

"Absolutely!" Liam shouted, when I asked about a spare couch to crash on. "Get up here. We need to get you back on the field."

He was right.

By the summer of 2007, Liam had already established himself as one of the best quarterbacks in Division I-AA football. He had sports reporters interviewing him and professional scouts dissecting his every pass. At that point in his career, he had twenty-four starts and thirty-six career touchdown passes. Me? I had zero games and zero pass receptions on my résumé.

But Liam had faith. He kept telling me how much he was looking forward to our finally playing together.

ON THE FOOTBALL field, I felt like I was ready to make an impact. But our receivers were good. Though

Liam had helped me learn some of Coach Brown's offensive scheme over the summer, I wasn't one of the top receivers coming out of camp.

Because of my academic situation, I wasn't allowed to suit up for the first five games of the 2007 season. I'd have to watch from the sideline, taking mental notes.

WITH *PAPÍ* AND MY FATHER GONE, I WAS NOW THE MAN OF THE HOUSE.

On October 1, I got a phone call from my mother.

Papí had passed away.

I went home the next day. I looked around my *abuela*'s apartment on East Twentieth and saw my grandmother, my mother, and my little sister staring back at me.

With *Papí* and my father gone, I was now the man of the house.

I promised myself I'd do my best to make those men proud.

NEARLY THREE YEARS after committing to play at UMass, I suited up for my first college football game on October 13, 2007. We were playing Villanova at home.

I only caught one pass the rest of the entire 2007 season, but it felt great to be a real part of the team.

That semester, I finally picked a major, African-

American history. My father was a proud African-American man who knew all about the challenges and achievements of the civil rights movement. I used his passion for the subject as motivation and dove into my schoolwork like never before. When my grades came in, I didn't cower in fear. I ran into the kitchen to share them with my mother and sister. I recorded two A's and two B's, bumping my cumulative GPA up to a 2.75.

The man of the house had turned things around.

HEADING INTO THE 2008 season, everybody wondered who'd replace the senior receivers we had lost to graduation. I had trained all summer, and it became obvious in those first weeks of training camp that Liam and I had something special going on.

Our third game of the 2008 season was against James Madison University, a conference rival of ours. On our first drive of the game, Liam hit me for a five-yard pass. On our next drive, we connected on a nine-yard out. I was feeling good, but we were down 31–10 at the half.

Liam pulled me aside in the locker room at halftime. "Vic, you can beat that guy who's covering you out there, right?"

I nodded. I always felt like I could beat anybody.

"Then what are we waiting for? Let's get started with that breakout year of yours."

In the second half, I caught eleven passes for 238 yards and scored two touchdowns. Everything Liam threw in my direction, I caught. Outs. Posts. Hooks. Everything.

We lost the game that afternoon, but I'd finally emerged onto the scene. My thirteen catches more than doubled my entire previous career reception total, while my 262 receiving yards almost tripled my career yardage numbers. Both statistics broke UMass school records for a single game.

Liam and I were in a groove all year long. By the end of the season, we'd both put up huge statistics. In 2008—my first real season playing college football—I led the team in receptions and receiving yards. Liam, meanwhile, shattered every UMass passing record there ever was and finished his four-year stint with ninety career touchdown passes.

At the end of the season, the team held a big football awards banquet. All of the players and their families were encouraged to attend. My mother and sister made the trip up from Paterson.

Not surprisingly, Liam won the Team MVP award. For four of his five years on campus, he *was* UMass football. I was thrilled to see his efforts recognized.

At the end of the night, Coach Brown took to the stage and announced the winner of one last award.

"This young man's overcome a lot of adversity, not only

in the past twelve months, but the past four years. A lot of kids would have given up on their dreams a long time ago. Others might have tried taking an easy way out. But this kid just kept on working. He kept on believing. Victor Cruz, please come up to the stage and accept the award for the Most Improved Player of 2008."

As I got up to walk to the podium, I noticed everyone getting up out of their seats.

It took a second to realize that the crowd was standing and clapping for *me*. It was the first and only standing ovation I've ever received.

A few weeks later, my grades came in the mail. I got a 3.0 that semester, bumping my cumulative grade point average to a 2.9.

My life was finally stable. Things were falling into place.

Papí would have been thrilled.

IN JANUARY 2009, Coach Brown announced that he was leaving UMass to take a position at the University of Maryland. Kevin Morris, our offensive coordinator, got promoted to head coach. With Liam planning to graduate that June, it was increasingly clear that I'd have to step up and become one of the leaders of the team.

I relished the opportunity. Along with fellow seniors Jeromy Miles and Vladimir Ducasse, I organized team workouts and weight-lifting sessions throughout the spring.

I became more vocal and set an example by being the first one to the gym in the morning and the last one to leave at night. It wasn't enough just to be a good player anymore. I wanted to be the guy the younger players looked up to.

That March, I received an e-mail from the UMass admissions office with the subject line "Victor Cruz: Academic Standing."

My heart sank.

What now? Had I enrolled in the wrong classes? Was there something wrong with my credits from PCCC? Was I being accused of breaking the honor code?

I opened the e-mail and was pleasantly surprised. It turned out that because of all the college credits I had picked up at Bridgton Academy, College County of Morris, and PCCC, I already had enough credits to graduate.

My academic adviser explained that I'd only have to take one course my senior year. As an African-American history major, I still needed to write a thirty-five-page senior thesis paper.

I'd never written a ten-page paper before. The thought of doing thirty-five pages was daunting. But just as I'd done with everything else those past few months, I decided to embrace the challenge and conquer it.

My senior thesis was titled "The African-American Male Athlete as Captured by the Media." I spent hours in the library, researching the different ways men like Jackie

Robinson, Muhammad Ali, and Jim Brown had been portrayed by the media during their playing days. I also tracked how national outlets had covered recent stories involving NFL stars Michael Vick and Adam "Pac-Man" Jones. I worked on that thesis throughout my senior year. I always knew I could catch footballs and score touchdowns if given the chance. But writing that paper was something a seventeen-year-old Victor Cruz would never have dreamed of doing. To conquer the task took patience, dedication, and ingenuity.

I got an A.

MY SENIOR SEASON was another strong one. I caught fifty-nine passes and scored five touchdowns. I scored twice in a big day against Albany. We faced Hofstra in the last game of my college career, and I had eleven receptions for 155 yards. I was named to the CAA All-Conference First Team, a tremendous honor, and finished fourth all-time on the UMass career receptions list. At our annual team banquet in January, I was chosen as the 2009 Team MVP.

I'd had a productive two years on the field, but the NFL might never have noticed me at all if not for my teammate Vladimir Ducasse.

A fellow senior in 2009, Vlad was a six-foot-five, 325-pound scientific anomaly. He was huge, but he was agile. NFL scouts were enamored with Vlad's physical build, and the way he flat-out dominated opposing defensive ends. And while they were watching him, they saw a little of me as well.

After the season, a local sports agent named Jack Huntington offered to pay for my NFL Draft training down in Bradenton, Florida. I signed on the dotted line and was sent to Athletic Edge Training Center, a performance facility where NFL Draft prospects prepare for tryouts.

In Bradenton, I trained with some of the best players in all of college football. Though I wasn't one of the 320 players invited to the NFL's annual Draft Scouting Combine that February, Jack assured me that I'd still have a chance to work out for all thirty-two teams before the NFL Draft in April.

In March, I was invited to Boston College's NFL Pro Day. Scouts from fourteen NFL teams planned to gather on BC's campus to watch about thirty NFL Draft–eligible players from the area work out.

Because of a blizzard, we were all sent to Harvard's indoor facilities in Cambridge. With thirty scouts watching, I ran the all-important forty-yard dash in 4.42 seconds. It was the fastest I'd ever run the forty. I then hit the bench press and did sixteen reps of 225 pounds.

I had an incredible workout. Jack said I was suddenly an NFL Draft "sleeper," a little-known prospect who had all the NFL scouts and media "draftniks" buzzing.

The New York Giants hosted a local Pro Day in early April at the Timex Center in East Rutherford. The work-out session consisted of all the guys who attended college in the New Jersey and New York area and some players from Philadelphia and Connecticut. Since I was living at home in Paterson, Jack suggested I attend. I came and performed well in front of the Giants scouts.

The NFL Draft was at the end of the month. Accord-ing to Jack, the Carolina Panthers were interested in me. "They could take you in the sixth or seventh round, but you'll most likely have to try out for their team as an undrafted rookie free agent."

Jack found news like that encouraging, but I was disap-pointed. I couldn't understand why no teams were sold on me. Sure, I didn't put up huge statistics at UMass, and no, I wasn't built like six-foot-five Calvin Johnson. But I wanted it so badly. Somebody just had to take a chance on me.

A few days before the 2010 NFL Draft, Jack called to say that a new team had inquired about me.

"The New York Giants have a scout, a guy named Chris Pettit, who really likes what you bring to the table."

The Giants, huh?

I'd grown up fifteen miles from Giants Stadium but had never once stepped foot in the building. I had always been a fervent Dallas Cowboys supporter. The Giants were the enemies. When they beat the Cowboys in the NFC Divisional Round of the 2007 playoffs, I threw the TV remote control across our living room on East Eighteenth Street.

I hated the Giants.

Then I started to daydream about what it would be like to play for a local NFL team. Would my mother and Elaina get to attend all of my home games? Would the sports bars in Clifton put my jersey up on their walls? Would I be considered a "Hometown Hero" and loved by the fans?

On the Tuesday morning before the 2010 NFL Draft, I sat at the computer in my bedroom. I clicked on the New York Giants logo, scrolled down to the roster tab, and looked at their wide receivers.

The Giants were loaded.

In total, they had eight different wide receivers. Maybe I'd gotten excited over nothing. With so many veteran players under contract, there was no need for the Giants to add *another* wide receiver to the mix.

Out of curiosity, I decided to check out the other team that had expressed interest in me—the Carolina Panthers. I printed out their roster and took out a yellow highlighter pen. Which of their wide receivers could I compete with for a spot on the roster?

Then I decided to do the same thing with the Dallas Cowboys. And then the Jets. And the Colts. Brandon Marshall had just been traded from the Broncos to the Dolphins. Maybe Denver needed a new receiver? I printed out their roster and marked it up with the highlighter.

Six hours later, my bedroom looked like a mad scientist's laboratory. I had all thirty-two NFL teams' rosters printed out, marked up, and spread out everywhere. By dinnertime, I had Post-it notes all over my wall too.

Before I went to sleep, I clicked on a popular website called NFLDraftScout.com. I discovered that I was ranked as the seventy-third-best wide receiver prospect in the 2010 NFL Draft. The league only had thirty-two teams.

Seventy-third.

I typed out the names, schools, heights, weights, and forty-yard-dash times of all seventy-two receivers who were ranked above me.

I started to get fired up. I did a set of push-ups on the floor. I followed that with five hundred sit-ups.

Around midnight, my mother walked into my bedroom. She took in the scattered paperwork and the enraged look in my eyes. "If only you had worked this hard during your freshman year of college," she laughed.

Even I had to smile at that one.

The NFL Draft was a painstakingly long, three-day experience. I ordered a pizza and sat alone on my couch for the entire first round. I watched every pick with the understanding that my name probably wouldn't be called. Still, I thought there was a chance.

There wasn't.

The second day consisted of rounds two and three. Jack told me it'd be a "pleasant surprise" if any team selected me in either of those rounds. Still, I kept my hopes up.

Two hours into the evening, the New York Jets were on the clock with the sixty-first pick. I was fixing something in the kitchen when I heard a familiar name announced on the TV.

"The New York Jets have selected Vladimir Ducasse, an offensive guard out of the University of Massachusetts Amherst."

I was thrilled for Vlad. He'd been a great teammate, and all of his hard work had paid off. I sent him a text message saying "Congratulations," and he wrote back, almost immediately, "Thanks, Vic. You're up next!"

The rest of the night went by without my name being called. "It's out of our hands, Vic," Jack told me afterward. "Now try to get some sleep."

But I didn't. I just stared at the ceiling in my bedroom and thought about my life. I thought about those days in The Sir's dojo. I thought about doing pull-ups with my father in Montgomery Park. I thought about summer mornings running routes with Liam in Amherst.

The third day of the draft covered rounds four through seven. Jack told me he'd call if he had any news.

I didn't hear from him.

The Detroit Lions had the 255th and final selection in the 2010 NFL Draft. I looked at their roster, marked up with yellow highlighter pen in front of me. There was a chance, I thought, that they'd draft a wide receiver.

They did.

But his name wasn't Victor Cruz. His name was Tim Toone. A five-foot-ten guy from a school called Weber State, Tim Toone was the twenty-seventh receiver and the final player taken in the 2010 NFL Draft.

A few seconds after the ESPN NFL Draft crew bid their viewers farewell, my phone rang. "Victor," said Jack, "I've got some good news."

I was all ears.

"Three teams want you to try out for them. The Carolina Panthers, the Denver Broncos, and the Washington Redskins are all interested in bringing you in as an undrafted rookie free agent. You're going to have to pick one of those three teams tonight."

My head was spinning. Jack explained that for undrafted guys like me, the three hours after the NFL Draft were crucial. Teams called up all the agents of the players they still had interest in and offered the players a tryout. If you impressed the team in the tryout, you'd get an invitation to training camp. If you impressed the team in training camp, you could make the regular season roster.

It sounded like a million steps away from actually suiting up in an NFL game, but I was ready.

I looked at the three team rosters and started weighing the pros and cons of living in North Carolina, Denver, and Washington, D.C. I called Elaina up and asked her what she thought.

Just as I was getting ready to give Jack an answer, he called again.

"Vic, forget Carolina, Denver, and Washington," he shouted into the phone. "The New York Giants just offered you a contract, kiddo! You don't have to try out either. They're skipping all that. You got an invite to training camp!"

Jack explained that the scout who liked me, Chris Pettit, had gone to bat for me. He had assured the other scouts, the coaching staff, and the Giants front office that I'd make it worth their investment.

I'd only met Chris Pettit once in my life. He'd introduced himself at the UMass Pro Day. We exchanged brief hellos and didn't even have a real conversation. If I'd been asked, I couldn't have picked him out of a lineup.

But at that moment, I was ready to walk to Chris Pettit's house, wherever he lived, and give him a giant hug.

GOING IN

THE FIRST DAY of Giants rookie minicamp felt like my first day of school at Paterson Catholic. I had dreamed of entering an NFL locker room for so long that when it finally happened, nothing in the world could wipe the little kid smile off my face.

Well, one guy could.

"I'm Coach Tom Coughlin" were the first words I heard from the longtime head coach of the New York Giants. "And I don't care if you were a first-round pick, a second-round pick, a high school superstar, or the greatest thing to ever step foot on your college campus. You're a rookie on the New York Giants now. You're at the very bottom of the barrel. I hope you're ready to work."

I didn't say one word to Coach Coughlin during that rookie minicamp. Partly, it was because I decided to let my actions speak for themselves. I was also too terrified of the man even to introduce myself.

Coach Coughlin wasn't the most physically imposing person, but he carried himself like a true leader of men. When he walked into a room, everyone stopped talking.

He didn't waste his words, and he never gave one player special treatment over another.

I couldn't wait to show Coach Coughlin everything I had. I couldn't wait to *give* him everything I had to give. I was ready to do whatever it took to be a part of his football team.

There were some real characters in the Giants 2010 rookie class. Jason Pierre-Paul had been the team's first-round pick in April. I'd never heard of him in college, but when I had typed his name into YouTube before the draft, a video of him doing seventeen consecutive backflips was the first thing that came up.

I COULDN'T WAIT TO SHOW COACH COUGHLIN EVERYTHING I HAD.

I roomed with another undrafted rookie wide receiver, a kid from Memphis with a thick Southern accent named Duke Calhoun. Duke had done some special things in college, but like me, he wasn't one of the twenty-seven receivers drafted in April.

Duke was a bit embarrassed to confess that he'd never heard of me. I said it wasn't a problem. Then I promptly rattled off his height, weight, forty-yard-dash time, and the fact that NFLDraftScout.com had ranked him as the thirty-fourth-best wide receiver in the 2010 NFL Draft.

My *abuela* (grandmother), who taught me the salsa dance and so much more, always kept me smiling.

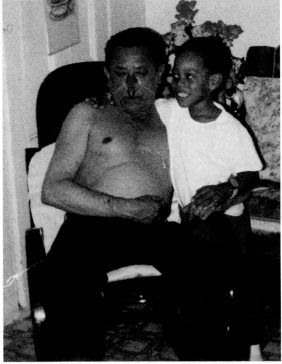

Papí, her husband, was my first best friend, and he gave me a love of music, wrestling, and adventure.

Above: My father, Mike Walker, with his two sons, my brother, Malik, and me.

Left: Dad was always proud of my tae kwon do championships. How about those glasses?!

Right: The first football team I played for was the PAL North Firefighters. I didn't play receiver. I played center. My dad was sometimes my coach but always my biggest fan.

Above: Tae kwon do was my first passion. Long before I was hauling in touchdowns, I was mastering the flying roundhouse kick.

Left: First-place finishes always felt great.

Right: Malik and I were competitors on the basketball court. One of the craziest days was when we went up against each other in high school. Dad didn't pick sides.

My dad and me after we won the state title my senior year of high school. He never missed a game.

Coach Wimberly, a Paterson legend, who was not just my first coach but one of my first real mentors.

With Mom and Dad signing my letter of intent to attend the University of Massachusetts–Amherst.

Before I even touched the football field at Paterson Catholic, I was the point guard on the hoops team. My chief responsibility? Getting my teammates the ball.

I met Elaina one month before I left for prep school; she's been by my side ever since.

I was always proud to wear my UMass jacket. Here I am during those years with my little sister Andrea.

My mother is the strongest woman I know. She's been with me through all the ups and downs, and I wouldn't be where I am today without her.

Top left: Keep your eye on the ball because you never know where it's going to land.

Top right: Eli Manning, not only a good quarterback but one of the elite pass throwers in the game.

Right: My big breakout game, a three-touchdown performance against the Jets on *Monday Night Football*.

Below: Doing the salsa dance after my first NFL touchdown was great, but beating the Dream Team Eagles in Philadelphia was what mattered most.

Saying a prayer before the Patriots game. *Papí* and my dad are with me on every play.

Our Christmas Eve game against the Jets was make or break for the season. If we had lost, our chances at the playoffs would have been slim to none.

My ninety-nine-yard touchdown reception against the Jets saved our season and cemented my place in the Giants' record books. It made for an incredible Christmas weekend.

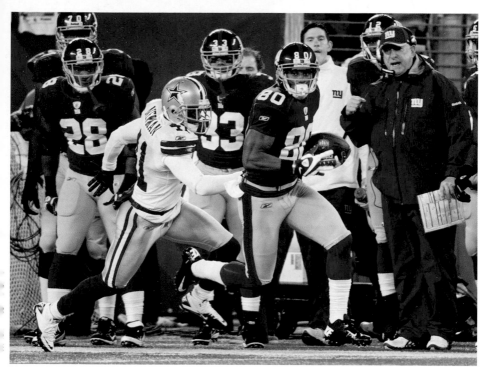

I grew up a Dallas Cowboys fan, but I had no problem contributing to eliminating them from playoff contention.

Our 31–14 win over the Cowboys clinched the NFC East. In front of our home crowd, nothing felt sweeter.

Right: James Ihedigbo took me around on my campus tour when I visited UMass as a high school senior. Eight years later, two undrafted "small school" guys went at it on the biggest of stages in the Super Bowl.

Below: Giants fans are incredible. They were out in full force in Green Bay.

Top: Doing my best Michael Irvin impression, signaling for a first down against the Patriots in Super Bowl XLVI.

Left: Getting another shot against Carlos Rogers, the guy who outplayed me in week ten in the NFC championship game.

Touchdown!

Hoisting the Lombardi Trophy with my teammate, friend, and fellow receiver Hakeem Nicks.

Celebrating the big win with my brother, Malik, and my sister Ebony.

Marching down the Canyon of Heroes with my Giants teammates. Twelve months earlier I wasn't even sure I'd make the team.

Back in Paterson getting a hero's welcome with friends and family.

Move the chains! My story's still being written. It's first and ten with the rest of my life ahead of me.

Duke shook his head and asked me if I was crazy.

I told him I was.

ALL THE VETERANS and free agent camp invitees reported to the University of Albany for training camp on August 1. The first time I walked into our locker room, I saw a blue jersey hanging on a locker with the number 3 and the last name Cruz on the back.

I took a moment before putting that jersey on.

It was more than just my first NFL jersey. It was a symbol of my roots. That jersey identified my *abuela*, my mother, and their incredible journey to America. I'd wear that jersey with more pride than anything I'd ever worn before.

Training camp was hard work, but I enjoyed the competition. Every day, we'd go out on the field and work our tails off. In addition to all the rookies and free agent invitees, the veterans on the team had no guarantees. They were also trying to make the squad again.

There were a lot of talented wide receivers in camp that summer. My goal each day was to make one play—a catch, a block, or a special teams tackle—that would help me stand out from the pack.

Every night after practice, I'd go back to my dorm room and call Elaina. I'd brag about a one-handed grab or tell her something positive a coach had said to me.

"Stay humble, Vic," she'd tell me. "You haven't made the team yet."

A week into training camp, though, I was making plays and turning heads. At the same time, some of the other receivers on the team were nursing injuries. Steve Smith, Mario Manningham, and Hakeem Nicks—the top three receivers on the Giants—all missed significant time during training camp. That gave guys like Duke and me the chance to show what we could do.

On one particular afternoon practice session, I made a move at the line of scrimmage and ran right past starting cornerback Terrell Thomas for a deep pass completion.

The Giants fans in attendance that day, many of whom had seen me play against Albany during my senior season at UMass, responded with a loud chant of "Cruuuuuuuz."

It was the first time I'd ever heard my name chanted.

Though I still hadn't said a word to Coach Coughlin, he came up after the practice and patted me on the rear end. "Nice job today, son," he said.

IT WAS THE FIRST TIME I'D EVER HEARD MY NAME CHANTED.

Our first preseason game was against the Jets at the new MetLife Stadium in East Rutherford. During pregame warm-ups, I looked around the stadium, trying to soak it all in. Elaina and my mother were both in the building,

Coach Wimberly and Jim Salmon were coming together, and the game was going to be on in every bar and restaurant in Paterson.

Our teams went back and forth throughout the first two quarters. At halftime, the Jets held a 13–10 lead.

With three minutes left in the third quarter, Kevin Gilbride, the Giants' offensive coordinator, signaled to me on the sideline. "Cruz, you're going in."

Jim Sorgi was in at quarterback, and the play had me running a straight Go route. Dwight Lowery, a five-foot-eleven cornerback, was lined up against me in man-to-man coverage. Jim took three steps back, looked in my direction, and lofted a pass toward me on the left side of the field. My right arm got tied up with Lowery's left, leaving me with just one arm to make a play. As the ball began its descent from the sky, I had only one option—to grab the ball with one hand.

It was a catch I'd made in countless high school and college practices. But never in a game. I stretched my left arm out, kept my eyes open, and hoped for the best. When I felt the ball land perfectly in my left palm, I cradled it like a baby, tucked it against my hip, and refused to let go. I heard the roar of the crowd and saw Dwight Lowery on the ground beneath me. I skipped away from his grasping arms and caught a glimpse of what was ahead of me— nothing but an open field.

I remember thinking, Don't fall, Vic. Don't fall.

As I crossed the ten yard line, I realized I was going to score a touchdown on my first NFL reception. I glided past the goal line, placed the ball on top of the Jets logo, and turned around to see my teammates jumping up and down.

When I got back to the sideline, Coach Gilbride patted me on the behind and asked, "Got another one in you, Cruz?"

"Absolutely, Coach," I replied.

On our next offensive drive, Jim Sorgi drove us down the field with a few short completions to our running backs. On second and seven from our own thirty-nine yard line, Jim took another three-step drop and whizzed a pass my way. Lowery was draped all over me, but when I saw Jim's toss was going to come up short, I fought off Lowery and came back to the ball. As I caught the pass, I danced past him, pushed myself off another Jets player, and picked up seven more yards. First down.

Two plays later, the Jets replaced Lowery with a longtime NFL starting cornerback named Drew Coleman. As we squared off at the line of scrimmage, Coleman said, "Sorry, man. You're not catching any more balls tonight."

Before I could even think about responding, Jim threw a perfectly lobbed ball aimed my way along the sideline.

I fought past Coleman, made a strong cut toward the outside, and stretched out my arms.

The ball landed perfectly in my hands and I jogged into the end zone.

Another touchdown.

On our next possession Rhett Bomar was in at quarterback. Like me, Rhett was doing everything he could to make the team. On his first pass, Rhett threw me a five-yard slant for a short gain. A few plays later, he hit me on a sixteen-yard crossing route. After a couple more first downs, it was first and goal from the five yard line.

Rhett looked at me in the huddle. "Vic, we've been practicing this play together all summer. Back shoulder fade. Let's go."

He took the snap, backpedaled a few steps, and threw a perfect pass over my right shoulder. I reached up, hauled the ball in, and landed in the end zone. Touchdown.

As I jogged back to the sideline, the reality of the situation started to dawn on me. In my first game in an NFL uniform, I'd just caught six passes for 148 yards and scored three touchdowns. More importantly, when I had entered the game, we were losing 16–10. When the final whistle blew, we'd won 31–16.

I MET ELAINA, my little sister, and my mother in the parking lot afterward and we drove home to Paterson. We were all smiling, but were just too shell-shocked by what had occurred to really discuss the game yet.

Then, as we got on Route 3 and headed into Paterson, Elaina spoke up. "Vic, have you checked your Twitter?"

"Nah. Are there people talking about the game?" I assumed there might be some chatter because the game had been on ESPN.

"Victor, LeBron James was tweeting about you tonight."

Excuse me? LeBron James?

Apparently, after my second touchdown grab, Miami Heat forward LeBron James had tweeted to his four *million* Twitter followers: "Victor Cruz going nuts on the Jets tonight on #MNF. Undrafted rookie from UMass. He's gonna have a job this year for sure."

I smiled. "I hope he's right."

The next morning, I was ready to get back to the practice field. Obviously, it felt great to score three touchdowns on national television, but I was still the seventh or eighth receiver on the depth chart. The Giants never kept more than seven receivers. I'd need to do far more if I wanted to make the squad.

When I got to my locker after Wednesday's practice, a mob of reporters was waiting to speak with me.

"Victor," one of the local beat reporters began, "during Monday night's ESPN broadcast, Jon Gruden said that you were an *American Idol* story. He said that you had come 'out of nowhere.' Any thoughts?"

"I'm flattered by all that," I said, "and I respect Coach Gruden's opinion. But I really haven't come from 'out of nowhere.' I'm from Paterson, New Jersey—just a few miles away."

Pat Hanlon, the Giants longtime public relations director, swooped by my locker and leaned in toward my ear. "Hell of an answer, kid," he whispered. "I couldn't have written it better myself."

The New York media was enjoying their "Victor Cruz: From Rags to Riches" story line, but Jack and Elaina kept me grounded.

We played the Steelers the following week, and I had just two catches for thirty yards. It was disappointing. Two catches for thirty yards wasn't going to get me on the Giants.

Our third preseason game was on the road against the Baltimore Ravens. Again, I didn't enter the game until late in the third quarter. "Don't be too concerned about *when* you're put in," Coach Ryan, our receivers coach, told me at halftime. "Just be ready to be special when your number *is* called."

With a little under seven minutes remaining in the third quarter, Coach Gilbride waved me over. "Hey, Cruz," he screamed, "go make something happen."

On third and two from our own twenty-one yard line, Rhett threw me a twenty-yard pass toward the Ravens' sideline. Initially, it seemed out of my reach. I lunged forward, stretched my arms out as far as I could, and grabbed the ball with my fingertips. Thirty-five yards. First down. It was our biggest pass play of the night.

For the casual NFL fan, the fourth quarter of a preseason game might not seem very interesting. But for an undrafted rookie fighting to make the team, the fourth quarter of a preseason game feels like the Super Bowl. Every single play is an opportunity to prove to the coaches that you matter, that you're an indispensable part of the team.

I pulled Rhett aside before we began our final drive and looked at him straight in the eye. "Rhett, we've worked all summer to make this team," I said. "Now let's *make this team*."

The scoreboard read 24–3, and the stadium had already emptied out. But that final drive meant everything in the world. On first and ten, Rhett hit me on a short pass to the right. I made a move on the cornerback and darted twenty-four yards for a big gain. A couple of plays later, I linked eyes with Rhett one more time. "Again," I said sternly. "Again, Rhett!"

Rhett didn't smile or object; he just nodded.

He went back three steps and tossed me a dart right in

my numbers. I hauled the pass in, made the man covering me miss, and bolted a few more yards for the first down.

On the next play, he connected with my rookie mini-camp roommate, Duke Calhoun, for a twenty-yard pass completion.

It was now first and goal from the one yard line. I wanted the ball.

Rhett set up in a shotgun formation, took the snap, and threw a high, floating fade pass toward the back of the end zone.

I had to make this catch.

I snuck behind the Ravens cornerback and extended my arms high into the sky. When my fingertips felt the football, I secured it with all of my might. My feet were in. Touchdown.

We eventually lost 24–10, but I'd made an impact. I had led the team in receptions, receiving yards, and had scored our only touchdown of the evening.

Our fourth and final preseason game was home against the New England Patriots. Before the game, the tension ran high in the locker room. Many of us knew this would be the last time we ever put on a New York Giants uniform.

I caught three passes, including a twenty-four-yarder from Rhett in the second quarter, and felt good about my final audition for the squad. Still, when I left MetLife Stadium that night, my future felt uncertain. Had I done enough to catch the eye of General Manager Jerry Reese or the coaching staff? I couldn't say. Of the seventy-five players who had arrived at training camp, only fifty-three of us would make the final roster. The only thing I knew for sure was that I had given the New York Giants my absolute everything.

Earlier in the summer, D. J. Ware, a running back who'd bounced from team to team over his first three years in the league, had explained what would happen next.

"You sit and you wait," he said. "Remember NFL Draft day? It's like that all over again, but it's the exact opposite. You don't want that phone ringing. If you get a phone call, it means they're calling you to come in and turn in your playbook."

The Sunday morning after the Patriots game was "Cut Day." I had a long talk with Elaina. She was the love of my life and my biggest fan. We looked at the different wide receivers on the roster and discussed my chances of making the team.

The Giants had kept six receivers on their active roster in 2009. Most likely, there was just one spot left to fill on the 2010 squad. It would come down to me, Duke, Tim Brown, and veteran wide receiver Derek Hagan. We'd all played well that summer, and we offered different skill sets to the team.

"You did all you could," Elaina told me. "You've already made everybody so proud."

The hours went by and I heard nothing.

Then I got a text message from Rhett Bomar: "Hey, buddy, it was an honor playing with you this summer. They just cut me. Hoping to get a contract somewhere else."

A few minutes later, I got a text from Tim Brown: "Just got the call. Headed in there now."

Soon after that, I found out that the Giants had also cut Derek Hagan.

It was a strange feeling. These were guys I'd come to know and love over the past several weeks. But each one of their releases improved my chances of making the team. I felt terrible for them, but at the same time optimistic about my own future.

More hours came and went.

At around seven p.m., the phone finally rang. It was Sean Ryan, our receivers coach.

"What's up, Coach?" I asked, knowing my future as a New York Giant had already been determined.

"Congratulations, Victor," he said. "You've made the fifty-three-man roster. Come down to the facilities tomorrow and we'll get you situated. Our first game is in a week versus the Carolina Panthers. No time to celebrate. Be ready to hit the ground running."

I dropped the phone and ran into the other room to find Elaina.

"I made it!"

She hugged me and screamed so loud that I'm still shocked the neighbors didn't call the police.

I'd done it.

I knew it was just the start of my NFL career, but it meant so much on so many levels. Beyond the football, it'd change things in my life. I was being paid enough money to move out of my mother's home and into a new apartment with Elaina. I could also help pay for my little sister's college tuition.

As I sat on the front stoop of my mother's house, I noticed a pack of kids playing touch football in the street. I watched those boys play for twenty minutes, each one of them trying his best to make the other guys miss.

I'd be playing that sport for a living. I'd be getting paid to do what I truly loved.

I ARRIVED AT practice the next day eager to start my NFL career. Even though I had made the roster, nothing was guaranteed. I could be released at any point in the season if I wasn't playing well or to make room for another player.

Before our first regular season game, Coach Coughlin let me know that I'd be listed as "inactive." I'd get to dress and run out on the field with the team, but I wouldn't be getting any playing time in the game. He made sure I knew that it wasn't a reflection of the way I'd been practicing or any sort of knock against me as a player. It was just a coaching decision. We won 31–18 and were off to a promising start to the season.

The next week was a Sunday night affair versus the Colts in Indianapolis. It marked my first appearance in an NFL regular season game. I played on the special teams unit, chasing down punts and kickoffs, and blocking for our return man, Darius Reynaud.

Eli's older brother Peyton carved up our defense, and we were blown out of the building in a 38–14 loss. The following week, the Tennessee Titans beat us 29–10 in MetLife Stadium.

We were 1-2 and the Giants fans weren't happy. All week, I heard callers complaining about our effort on the sports radio shows.

"You can't listen to that stuff," Deon Grant told me. "If you are getting caught up with what guys are saying in a recording studio somewhere, you're not focusing on what really matters."

He was right.

I had a job to do, and on the next Monday night we'd be playing in a pivotal game against the 3-0 Chicago Bears.

All week, we prepared for Chicago's All-Pro punt return

specialist, Devin Hester. Our special teams coach, Tom Quinn, instructed us to keep him contained any time he touched the football. During the game, our punt coverage unit silenced Hester, and our defense sacked Chicago's quarterbacks ten times. At the end, we wrapped up our second victory of the season, 17–3.

I was starting to get more comfortable with Coach Gilbride's offense, and I actually worked with the starting unit quite a bit in practice. The following week, we beat the Houston Texans, 34–10, improving our record to 3-2.

The Monday after the Houston game, I was running wind sprints before practice when I suddenly felt a sharp pain shooting down my right hamstring. It was as if I'd been stung by a million bees at once.

"You okay, Cruz?" my teammate Hakeem Nicks asked as I fell to the ground.

I thought I was fine, and nodded. When the training staff noticed me limping around, they urged me to get off the field.

In all my years playing competitive sports, I'd never once gotten hurt. I couldn't imagine I had really done anything too serious just running some sprints.

But the pain wasn't going away.

Initially, the doctors thought I had strained my hamstring. I was told I'd be back at full speed by the end of the week. When Friday came, though, I was still in tremendous pain. I couldn't walk.

I was listed as "inactive" for our next game, a matchup against the Lions. I focused on getting healthy for the week seven battle against the Cowboys. I'd had that one circled on the calendar since the rookie minicamp.

Unfortunately, when the doctors looked at my hamstring again, my greatest fear was confirmed. I hadn't just strained my hamstring; I had torn it.

"So, how long will I be out, Doc? Another two weeks? A month?"

Dr. Russell Warren, the Giants' lead physician. shook his head. "It means you're likely done for the year, Victor. I'm sorry."

And just like that, my 2010 season was over.

I'd made the team, but in five weeks with the Giants, I had zero catches, had zero yards, and scored zero touchdowns.

I'd have to wait until next season.

Of course, there almost was no next season.

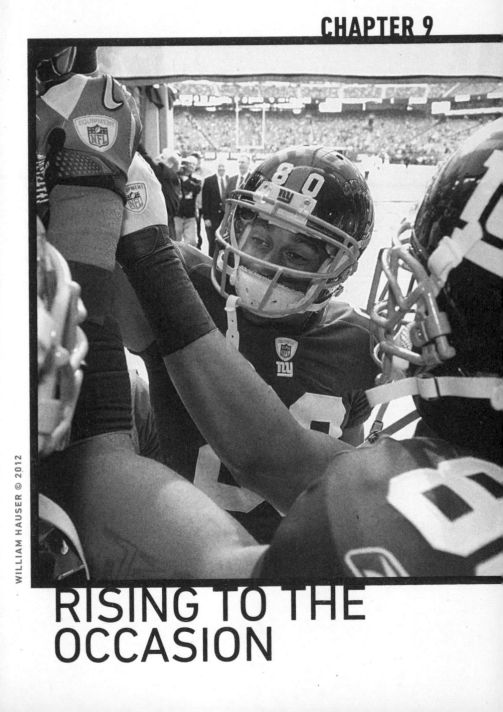

RISING TO THE OCCASION

I SPENT THE REMAINDER of 2010 rehabilitating my hamstring and watching the Giants compete from afar. I was still considered part of the team, but being on the injured reserve list meant my role was limited. I got to attend home games, but I couldn't travel to opposing stadiums.

The thought of being "Out of sight, out of mind" drove me wild. I'd see the other Giants receivers making spectacular catches or important plays on special teams and it'd burn me up inside. Of course, I was happy to see my teammates excelling. But the lingering thought of "That could have been me" would fester in my mind.

We had a 9-4 record heading into a week fifteen matchup with the Philadelphia Eagles. With a win, we'd be well positioned to make the NFC playoffs and perhaps a Super Bowl run.

But we lost the game 38–31.

The following week, the team traveled to Lambeau Field for a "must win" game against the Green Bay Packers. I watched that one from my apartment, alone on the couch, eating a bowl of cereal in my pajamas. We lost 45–17.

Not being able to do anything to help the team in either of those losses made for some long, sleepless nights.

We finished the season with a win in Washington, but our 10-6 record left us one victory shy of the playoffs.

THROUGHOUT THE 2010 regular season, there were whispers in our locker room about a potential NFL lockout that would postpone or, worse, cancel the upcoming 2011 season.

At the time I wasn't sure what all that would mean. But when the NFL lockout was announced in late March, the significance of the situation became strikingly clear.

In addition to not being able to communicate with the Giants coaches, team management, or office staff, I wouldn't be getting paid a dime until the lockout was lifted.

People assume that just because you wear an NFL uniform on Sundays, you're a multimillionaire, capable of buying fancy cars and summer homes on the beach. But my rookie contract wasn't for millions, and with the costs of moving into a new apartment, things were getting tighter as winter turned to spring.

I needed something to keep me occupied. So I focused on rehabilitating my hamstring. I linked up with a new physical trainer, a guy named Sean Donellan, and I hit the gym hard. I was ready to commit to whatever workout plan he had in mind. Every day I arrived early and stayed late. I thought about making the Giants during every exercise, stretch, and sprint.

The NFL Draft was held on April 30.

In the first round, the Giants took a cornerback out of Nebraska named Prince Amukamara. In the second, they selected Marvin Austin, a big defensive tackle. In the third, they drafted someone named Jerrel Jernigan.

"Jernigan's a five-ten, 190-pound speed demon who can really help out on special teams," one of the ESPN announcers explained. "Beyond Nicks and Manningham, the Giants don't have much depth at wide receiver. Jernigan will make for a great third wideout."

The next morning, I headed to the gym and elevated my off-season training to another gear. My hamstring still wasn't 100 percent, but I pushed myself harder than ever before. If the Giants were drafting Jerrel Jernigan—a receiver with a physical build and forty-yard-dash time nearly identical to mine—I had to respond. I became an animal in the gym, lifting weights and watching my diet as if I were training for a prizefight.

Then, one day in May, I got an e-mail from Eli Manning. It was addressed to the entire team and suggested we meet him at Hoboken High School for some informal workouts.

I got there at seven o'clock that first Wednesday morning and was pleased to see that I wasn't alone. Eli, Hakeem, Ramses, Duke, D. J. Ware, Kevin Boss, Sage Rosenfels, and veteran receivers Sam Giguere and Michael Clayton were all dressed and ready to go.

"If you go too long without playing football, you start to forget things," Eli told us as we stretched before taking the field. "Let's go through all the terminology, all of the routes, and be the most prepared offense in the league when the season starts in September.

"And, guys, I'm not thinking about the lockout right now," he added. "I'm confident that'll all work itself out."

Eli then paused for a moment and looked at each one of us. "I'm thinking about the Super Bowl."

We nodded. Though opening day was scheduled for the second Sunday in September, the 2011 New York Giants season started that morning in Hoboken.

We began going through all of our drills and went at it hard. One by one, kids would walk by the field, stop, and spend the rest of the day cheering us on. I made one particularly nice catch on a Curl route and heard a chant of "Cruuuuuuuz."

It'd been a while since I'd heard it, and I'd be lying if I didn't say that it sounded awfully good.

When the crowds of fans became too large, and the

media contingent too invasive, Eli moved our workout sessions to Bergen Catholic High School.

After one of our workouts there, Eli pulled me aside in the parking lot. "Hey, we're expecting big things out of you this year," he said. "I love the way you've come ready to work each morning. Keep it up during training camp."

I couldn't resist opening up to him. I told Eli how much it killed me to not be able to help more in 2010; how I had watched the Eagles' and Packers' losses from afar, feeling like I'd let the team down. I described how I felt when Jernigan was selected with the Giants' third-round pick.

"Hey, just use all that as fuel for your fire, man. Stay motivated. Stay hungry. You're playing well. Keep it up. Master the offense, and make a difference this year."

That parking lot chat was one of the first times Eli and I really connected on a one-on-one level.

ON JUNE 6, I started my day like I had started any other morning that summer. I made myself a bowl of cereal, went to the gym, and came home at eleven a.m. When I got back home, though, Elaina was sitting on the couch. She looked concerned.

"What's up, babe? Everything okay?"

"Vic, I've been feeling really weird lately," she said apprehensively.

All sorts of ominous questions raced through my mind. Had I done something wrong? Was she worried that I was still out of work? Was she breaking up with me?

"Vic," she said, and smiled. "I'm pregnant."

They were the most beautiful words I could ever have imagined hearing her say. I ran to the couch and gave her a hug and a giant kiss. It was amazing news.

"VIC," SHE SAID, AND SMILED. "I'M PREGNANT."

"When are you due?" I asked.

"Well, I'm at twelve weeks now. So I guess I'll be giving birth sometime in January."

"Perfect. Our baby will be able to watch Daddy in the Super Bowl!"

She punched me in the arm, and we both had a laugh. I then looked her in the eye and told her I loved her.

"I love you too," she replied.

I'd never been happier.

ON JULY 24, the team owners and the NFL Players Association finally resolved the labor situation. The lockout was over. Two days later, the NFL's free agency period opened with a flurry. Teams were free to retool their rosters, and the look and feel of several NFL franchises changed in a matter of days.

One move the Giants *didn't* make greatly affected my

chances of making the team. Steve Smith had been one of the team's top receivers for many seasons, but he had suffered a season-ending injury at the end of 2010, and the Giants had opted not to re-sign him.

With Steve out of the picture, I had no more excuses, no more numbers to compute. A spot on the 2011 Giants roster was mine for the taking.

A SPOT ON THE 2011 GIANTS ROSTER WAS MINE FOR THE TAKING.

I just had to earn it.

Because of the lockout, the 2011 training camp was much shorter than usual. With less opportunity to turn heads, I had to make an impact immediately.

My hamstring was back at full strength, and I was in the best shape of my life. Working with Eli all those mornings in May made for a smooth transition in August. We were on the same page on nearly every pass he threw me, and the rest of the team began to acknowledge our newfound chemistry.

"Hey, Cruz, did you and Eli have sleepovers during the lockout or something?" Brandon Jacobs joked, after we connected on a back shoulder fade.

When "Cut Day" rolled around forty-eight hours after our final preseason game, I didn't sit on the couch biting my nails like I had done the year before. I was confident that all my hard work had paid off and that the coaches would recognize the improvements in my overall game.

Coach Ryan called me at seven p.m., and I asked him the same thing I had a year ago: "What's up, Coach?"

He let me know that I'd made the squad and to be ready at the facilities the next morning. Before hanging up the phone, I told him that I was ready to do whatever was necessary to make the 2011 Giants a better football team.

OUR FIRST GAME was at Washington on the tenth anniversary of September 11. Only a few of the guys on the team knew my father had been a firefighter. I'm not sure any of them were aware that he had volunteered his services in Lower Manhattan in the days following 9/11.

When we rose for the National Anthem that afternoon, I looked around the stadium and savored the moment. There were close to a hundred thousand people in the building. But for those two minutes and twenty seconds, it was just Mike Walker and his son Victor—the NFL football player—taking it all in.

On our very first drive of the game, Coach Gilbride signaled for me on the sideline. "It's third and eight, Cruz," he shouted as I hustled toward him. "Go in there and get us the first down." This was it. I was finally being given the chance to show what I could do in a regular season game.

I ran my route, and Eli threw me a perfect pass. I planted my feet, extended my hands—and dropped the ball. It should have been an easy first down.

It was a terrible error and a momentum killer. When I got back to the sideline, Coach Gilbride was shaking his head. "Can't be dropping the easy ones, Cruz," he said. "I can't put you in the game if you can't catch them when they matter."

We lost the game 28–14, and Eli only threw one more pass in my direction the rest of the afternoon.

Hakeem was nursing a bruised knee throughout the following week in practice, and I'd been making plays in his absence. But on September 15, just four days before our next game against the St. Louis Rams, the Giants signed a deal with thirteen-year league veteran Brandon Stokley.

"You could do a lot worse than watching a guy who's made 330 career receptions," Coach Ryan told me after one of our weight room sessions that week. He was right. Brandon Stokley was my competition, but he came in and immediately showed me some of the tricks of the trade that he'd picked up over his long career.

Hakeem, Stokley, and I all dressed for the game with the Rams. In the third quarter, I entered the game in another big third-down situation. "Make a play! No drops this time," Coach Gilbride screamed as I jogged on the field.

As Eli was calling out orders at the line of scrimmage, I noticed that two Rams defenders were setting up on my side of the ball, ready to blitz him from his blind side. Though the play originally called for one pattern, I had to adjust to what I was now seeing on the field. Instead of going deep down the field, I'd have to run what's known as a "hot route" at the line of scrimmage. Eli would see that I'd read the blitz, and he'd get the ball out of his hands faster than usual. Once the pass came to me, I'd have to gain the extra yards for a first down.

Eli took the snap, both blitzers flew in, and he threw me a short pass at the line. I caught the ball, made my move, and lunged for the extra yardage.

First down!

When I got to the sideline, the coaches were all thrilled with the play. It was one thing to run a nice route and make a catch. It was an entirely other thing adapting to a blitz read at the line of scrimmage.

The truth was that I never would have been able to make that play had I not spent all those summer mornings practicing it with Eli. We had gone through that very situation on countless hot days. He'd explain, "Vic, if two guys come from this side in this protection, you have a hot route. If I call out 'Ricky, Ricky,' you don't have the hot route."

I made a lot of big catches in 2011, but that blitz read

in the third quarter against the Rams might have been the one I needed the most. We won the game 28–16 and I'd played a small, but notable, role.

Week three was a game many of us had circled on our calendars. Even before they signed half a dozen big stars in the off-season, we had a score to settle with the Philadelphia Eagles for the way they ruined our 2010 campaign.

Prior to the game, Coach Gilbride sat me down and told me that I'd be starting at wide receiver. Domenik Hixon had torn his ACL for the second straight year, in the game against the Rams, and Mario was still feeling the effects of a concussion. Though Stokley would get some action, he still wasn't as familiar with the offense as I was.

As I tried control my emotions and focus on the task ahead, Coach Sullivan, our quarterbacks coach, casually strolled over to my locker.

"You know, Victor, this month is Hispanic Heritage Month," he said, fully aware that Hispanic Heritage Month was the last thing on my mind a few hours before my first NFL start. "If you score a touchdown, you should do something to celebrate the month in the end zone."

Was he kidding? I was so nervous, I couldn't think straight, and here he was talking about an end zone celebration. I was just hoping to put on my pants the right way.

"Okay, Coach, I'll try," I said, deflecting the conversation and quickly returning to my playbook.

How would one even show Hispanic heritage in an end zone celebration? I loved my grandmother's cooking, but I wasn't going to pretend I was serving rice and beans after a touchdown.

Then it hit me.

I'd dance.

My *abuela* had taught me the salsa when I was about five years old. She had sat me down and said she was going to focus my energy into something fun. We did it all—the merengue, the bachata, and the samba. My favorite dance of all, though, was the salsa. She'd put on her favorite Tito Puente vinyl record and we'd dance for hours in the kitchen.

I'd seen Terrell Owens shake pom-poms, Joe Horn break out a cell phone, and Clinton Portis do a cartwheel, but no one had ever done the salsa in the end zone.

AFTER TAKING AN early 7–0 lead, we got the ball back deep in our own territory late in the first quarter. It was third and two, and Coach Gilbride gave me the same look he'd given me the week before against the Rams. It was time for me to make a play.

I jogged out onto the field. The man lined up across from me was inching toward the line of scrimmage, getting in position to blitz Eli. I ran five yards to the left, caught Eli's bullet pass, and shook off a tackle from Kurt Coleman, the Eagles' safety. I had the first down, but I wasn't done. After a few steps, I saw Nnamdi Asomugha—the Eagles' newly acquired All-Pro cornerback—coming my way.

I planted my left leg hard in front of me, shifted my hips to the right, and turned my entire body around. Asomugha lunged at me, but I slid out of his grasp. I took a hop step forward, realized I was past him, and saw nothing but the open field up ahead.

Only one Eagles defender had a chance to bring me down. When Hakeem threw a block on him at the ten yard line, I knew I would score. I crossed the goal line— and immediately thought of Coach Sullivan.

Should I really do this? I looked at the mass of Eagles fans, standing together, above the end zone. They were all booing and swearing at me.

Ah, why not?

I broke out in the very same salsa dance my grandmother had taught me on East Twentieth Street twenty years before.

Step, step, step. Move your arms. Shake your hips.

The salsa!

I jogged to the sideline, and the entire team was waiting for me.

Michael Boley, our starting linebacker, was laughing.

"What in the *hell* was that dance?" he asked.

Even Brandon Stokley, who never once did a touchdown celebration in his whole career, was smiling. "That was pretty good," he said as he slapped me on the back of the helmet.

Coach Sullivan was shaking his head with a smile from ear to ear. "I've seen a lot of crazy stuff over the years, Cruz," he laughed. "But that right there might take the cake."

The salsa end zone celebration was officially born.

But my afternoon wasn't done.

We were trailing 16–14 in the fourth quarter when Eli threw me a high, floating pass at the Eagles' goal line. As I readied myself for a leap, Nnamdi Asomugha grabbed me. His teammate Jarrad Page was in the area too. It was two-on-one, and I was the odd man out.

THE SALSA END ZONE CELEBRATION WAS OFFICIALLY BORN.

I jumped up when the ball hit its apex, and pulled it from the sky. As I was coming down, I remember thinking, Don't drop it, don't drop it.

I didn't. I landed on my feet and stretched the ball over the goal line. When the official swung his arms upright, giving the sign for touchdown, I jumped and pumped my fist. I didn't do the salsa, but I gave my teammate Henry Hynoski a powerful chest bump in the middle of the end zone.

We scored one more time, and left Philadelphia with a win. We were 2-1, tied for first place in the NFC East, and I'd played a major role in the victory.

My mother called that night to share some exciting news. "Your *abuela* heard about your salsa dance from all of her friends. She loves it. She wants you to do it every single time!"

Coach Sullivan got a kick out of that one. "See," he said, laughing. "I told you!"

HOMETOWN HERO

THE FOLLOWING SUNDAY, we traveled to the desert to play the Arizona Cardinals. Before the game, I was stretching at midfield when a player with a familiar face strolled past me.

I racked my brain. How did I know the guy? When had our paths crossed? Did we compete in college?

Then, as he turned his back, I saw his last name—Doucet.

Early Doucet was the physical freak of nature who had dominated the University of Virginia seven-on-seven football camp I had attended eight years before. Early had done things on a football field I'd never seen before.

Well, he had made it to the NFL.

But so had I.

We got off to a sluggish start and were trailing 27–17 late in the fourth quarter. Our offense took the field with less than five minutes remaining. "We can't afford a turnover here," Eli reminded us. "A turnover means the game is over."

On second and ten, Eli dropped back for a pass and threw a laser to Hakeem along the sideline for twenty-six yards. On the next play, he found our tight end, Jake Ballard, in the back of the end zone.

We'd cut the lead to 27–24 and needed a defensive stop. Our D responded, stuffing the Cardinals on three straight plays. We'd have one last opportunity to either tie or take the lead.

As we stood in the huddle with less than four minutes left, Eli repeated what he'd said before: "No turnovers. Hold on to the ball tightly. If we turn it over, we lose."

On first and ten, he took the snap out of the shotgun and rolled to his left. A defender came sprinting toward him, but Eli ducked, evading the sack. Free for an instant, he threw me a perfect pass twelve yards down the middle. I caught the ball, broke a tackle, and fell to the ground.

After I went down, I let go of the ball, already thinking about the next play. Yet, as I began to stand, a Cardinals player scooped up the football and ran with it the other way.

In college, once you go down, the play is over. In the pros, however, the ball remains in play until a defender touches you.

Before the Cardinals player could take the ball into the end zone, a series of whistles blew. Jerome Boger, the game's lead official, had called the play dead once I'd fallen to the ground. Ken Whisenhunt, the Cardinals' longtime head coach, threw out the red challenge flag, requesting a review of the ruling on the field.

The game went to a commercial break. During those three long minutes, I was too scared of Coach Coughlin and Coach Gilbride to even consider heading to the sideline. I'd made a tremendous error, recklessly dropping the football before being touched by an opponent.

As Boger emerged from the officials' huddle, I closed my eyes and held my breath.

"The ruling on the previous play was that the receiver gave himself up by going to the ground," he said into his microphone. "That cannot be challenged. First down, New York."

So it wasn't a fumble. It was a first down, and we were still alive!

On the very next play, Eli threw a beautiful twenty-nine-yard touchdown pass to Hakeem. Our defense stopped the Cardinals on their final drive, and we took a come-from-behind 31–27 win.

I could easily have been the biggest goat in all of New York City that week, but I wasn't. My teammates, of course, didn't let me get away with my careless play scot-free. Michael Boley, one of my closest friends on the team, teased me all week in practice. "Hold on to the ball, Cruz," he shouted from across the field. "Please!"

■ ■ ■ ■

THE NFL CAN be hard to figure out sometimes.

We were riding high after our big win in Arizona and got caught sleeping by Pete Carroll's 1-3 Seahawks, losing 36–25.

After that we faced the Buffalo Bills, who had jumped out to a surprising 4-1 start. Late in the fourth quarter, we were tied at 24. The Bills were driving the ball when Corey Webster, one of our starting cornerbacks, intercepted a Fitzpatrick pass deep in our own territory. With less than four minutes left in the game, Eli took the ball at our own nineteen yard line. A few Ahmad Bradshaw runs, a pair of pass interference penalties, and a Bear Pascoe reception got us within field goal range.

Lawrence Tynes, our kicker, booted one through the uprights to give us the three-point lead, and our defense sealed up the win.

Our record improved to 4-2, and we had our bye the following week.

With thirteen days before our next game, I finally had some time to relax and visit with my mother and little sister. I'd had some idea that everybody at home was cheering me on, but I hadn't realized just how proud everyone was of my success.

I took my mother to breakfast at the same IHOP restaurant we'd gone to a thousand times before, but this time was different. Kids were coming up to me, asking to pose for photographs. Grown men and women, people twice my age, were telling me how much joy I was giving them on Sundays.

I was flattered and a bit overwhelmed. I had lunch with Jim Salmon a couple of days later, and he helped put the situation in perspective. "Remember when you were thirteen years old, and you worshipped the ground Tim Thomas walked on?"

Of course. I wore my shorts like Tim Thomas, took jump shots like Tim Thomas, and even walked like Tim Thomas.

GROWN MEN AND WOMEN, PEOPLE TWICE MY AGE, WERE TELLING ME HOW MUCH JOY I WAS GIVING THEM ON SUNDAYS.

"You're the town's new Tim Thomas, Vic," he said, grinning. "These kids know where you're from and what you've overcome to get where you are today. They see all that and believe they have a chance to do the same. You may not realize it, but just by suiting up on Sundays and having fun, you're giving all of these kids hope."

It was a lot to take in.

Seeing the effect of my success on the town only made

me want to work harder. I wasn't just playing for myself, Elaina, and the bulge in Elaina's belly anymore.

I was playing for the thirteen-year-old kid at School 21 who thinks there's no other option than the streets. I was playing for the boy at the park who has to decide between a game of pickup hoops and an aluminum can of beer.

I was playing for Paterson.

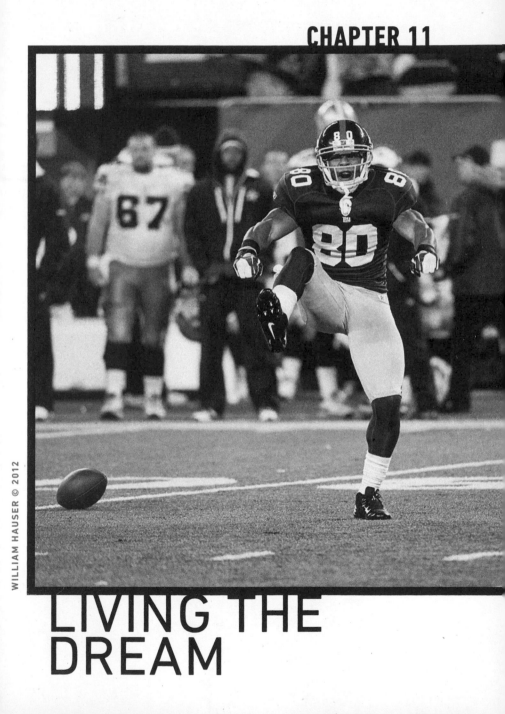

LIVING THE
DREAM

AFTER OUR WEEKEND off, we came out of the gates looking rusty in our week eight matchup with the Dolphins. Winless before the game, Miami jumped out to a 14–3 lead. But Eli hit Mario for a touchdown late in the second quarter, so we trailed 14–10 at the half.

The Dolphins added a field goal in the third quarter, leaving us seven points down. I'd had a few catches earlier in the game, but hadn't done anything special. As we jogged onto the field to start the fourth quarter, Eli looked at me and nodded.

He didn't have to say a thing.

On third and nine from our own twenty-seven yard line, Eli threw a deep pass to me over the middle of the field. I went up for the ball and grabbed it. First down. A few plays later, I made a seven-yard reception that put the ball in field goal range. After a Lawrence Tynes field goal, the Dolphins' lead was cut back to four.

Our defense came up huge, stopping the Dolphins on their next drive. We got the ball back with a little over eight minutes left in the game.

"Someone make a play for us," Coach Coughlin

pleaded as we took the field. Ahmad Bradshaw answered, scampering for a first down on second and eight. Eli then connected with Hakeem for a seventeen-yard completion. Two plays later, it was third and twelve from the Dolphins' twenty-five yard line.

Eli set up in the shotgun and gave me the look. It was coming to me.

He took the snap, I made a cut toward the middle, and he threw a bullet pass right in my numbers. As I caught the ball, I felt a Dolphins defender grab me with both arms from behind. Hoping to jar myself loose, I swung my body around 180 degrees. I felt the defender let go of my jersey. There was now just one man to beat. I sidestepped him with a shimmy move, and ran the ball in for a score. Touchdown.

ELI SET UP IN THE SHOTGUN AND GAVE ME THE LOOK. IT WAS COMING TO ME.

I did the salsa dance, and the crowd erupted with a "Cruuuuuuz" chant.

Our defense came up huge on the Dolphins' final two drives, sacking Matt Moore, Miami's quarterback, four times and intercepting his final pass of the game. It wasn't easy, but we had the W.

We were 5-2 with a trip to New England up ahead.

■ ■ ■ ■

THE PATRIOTS CAME into week nine having won their twenty previous regular-season home games. The streak dated back more than two complete NFL seasons.

None of that seemed to matter to the leaders in our locker room.

Eli, Brandon Jacobs, David Diehl, Justin Tuck, and Corey Webster were just some of the guys who'd played large roles in the 2007 team's upset win over the Patriots in Super Bowl XLII. All week during practice, the message from the veterans was the same: "Who cares about their streak? We've got their number. They're scared of *us*." It'd been more than three years since that game, but our team leaders remained confident. And their confidence was contagious.

Both offenses failed to get much going in the first half, leaving the score tied at 0-0. Our defensive game plan was working perfectly on Tom Brady, but we were having our own troubles. There were plenty of drops, penalties, and mental errors to go around.

In the fourth quarter, the Patriots took a 20–17 lead with less than two minutes remaining. I looked at Eli before we took the field for our final march of the game.

"You ready?" he asked, in the same even tone he would have used on any old question at any old time.

I strapped on my helmet and rubbed my hands together. "Yeah, I'm ready."

And then Eli went to work.

On first and ten, he hit me on a nineteen-yard pass play over the middle. First down. After two more throws in my direction, he connected with Jake Ballard for a clutch twenty-eight-yard gain on third down. We rushed to the line, and Eli quickly took the snap. I wasn't open and Mario was completely covered, so Eli cradled the ball under his arm and took off. We *never* saw Eli run. But there he was, with less than a minute to go, ripping off a twelve-yard gain for a first down.

Coach Coughlin called time-out, and the offense huddled on the sidelines. "Victor, I'm looking for you in the end zone," Eli told me. "Get to the goal line, and let's win this game."

As we lined up, I tried reading the defensive end. I knew that if I could break free in the play's first few seconds, I had a path to the goal line. Eli snapped the ball, and I dodged my way out of the defender's grasp. I looked up at around the five yard line and saw Eli winding up for a pass. As it came down from the air toward me, I was hit from behind. The ball dropped to the ground, but there was a yellow flag on the play.

Pass interference.

We got the ball on the one yard line with thirty seconds on the clock and a new set of downs.

On first down, Eli threw an errant pass to Ballard, and Brandon was stuffed at the line on second down. It was now third and one. We had no time-outs remaining.

Eli took the snap, faked a handoff to Brandon, and threw a dart off his back foot toward Ballard in the corner of the end zone. Jake stretched out his arms, caught the ball with both hands, and pulled it in for the score. Touchdown.

Our defense stuffed Brady in the game's final drive, and we all ran off the field, jumping up and down.

Even Coach Coughlin was smiling after the victory. He shook everyone's hand as we entered the locker room. Then, in a moment I'll never forget, we surrounded him and started jumping around like we were in a mosh pit. Michael Boley started chanting, "See you Wednesday! See you Wednesday!" and we all chimed in.

Usually we come to the facilities on Mondays to watch tape and get light workouts. Tuesdays are our off-days. But after rare wins or particularly tough road trips, Coach Coughlin would give us both days off.

"Now, listen," Coach Coughlin said "You are nine-point underdogs and there's *no way* you can win," he shouted, repeating what all of the talking heads had said before the game.

We all cheered.

"We've got a *good* football team," he continued. "And when we play together like that, and when we have a physical nature to the game, and we believe in ourselves that we're never out of it . . . well, that's a hell of a win."

We cheered again.

"You've got to come in and lift tomorrow, but I'll see you on Wednesday."

The locker room erupted.

THE SAN FRANCISCO 49ers were 7-1 and the hottest team in the league. They played physical defense and ran the ball hard up the middle behind a punishing offensive line.

Both offenses struggled in the first half as we exchanged field goals. Less than a minute before halftime, Eli threw me a pass toward the middle of the field. I broke to my right, but the ball was beyond me.

Carlos Rogers, San Francisco's top cornerback, got a good step on the play and intercepted the pass. I grabbed him from behind and made the tackle. As I was on the ground, I looked above me and saw a circle of 49ers players surrounding Rogers.

Then with his teammates cheering him on, he did a sarcastic salsa dance over me.

The 49ers then beat us 27–20.

After the game, we all sat at our lockers in disbelief. We'd been red hot the past few weeks, but we had come up short in our toughest battle to date.

AFTER A LONG flight home, a few of my friends suggested we go out and celebrate my twenty-fifth birthday. After some back-and-forth, a bunch of us headed into Manhattan for a Tuesday night out on the town. When we got to the spot, a place called Juliet Supper Club on West Twenty-first Street, there were a few tables in the corner set aside for our crew.

Elaina didn't make the trip in, so I spent the bulk of the night just hanging out and catching up with my boys. At around midnight, a bunch of the guys on the team said good-bye and headed home.

I stayed a little longer. We were off on Tuesdays, and with no curfew—I thought I had earned a night off to celebrate.

There were bottles, celebrities, and a DJ playing a great set. The way I saw it, getting home at one in the morning or getting home at three in the morning wasn't going to make any difference.

Then, at two thirty a.m., I heard gunshots.

Wap-wap-wap!

Unfortunately, it was a sound I knew all too well.

"Get down!" I shouted. In an instant, everyone in my party ducked for cover.

A second round of shots was fired.

As women were screaming and men were pushing to get out the front door, I sat under a table, frozen.

Everything was going so right in my life. I'd made it to the NFL, Elaina was seven months pregnant, and I was representing my family and my town better than I could ever have imagined.

And yet, here I was—sitting under a table during a nightclub shoot-out.

I waited for the chaos to finish.

When it did, I left the Juliet Supper Club with a new outlook. My life—and all the new responsibilities that came with it—was simply too valuable to be put at risk anymore. I'd done nothing wrong or illegal, but I decided there'd be no more nights out in New York—or anywhere, really—until two thirty in the morning.

The next day, I learned that a man had been shot and killed in the gunfight.

I showed up to practice knowing I'd have to explain myself to Coach Coughlin.

What I didn't expect was a mob of reporters waiting for me at my locker.

Almost four years earlier, Giants receiver Plaxico Burress had brought an unlicensed gun into a New York City nightclub and accidentally shot himself in the leg. It was a national news story and a black eye for both Burress and the New York Giants.

THE NEXT DAY, I LEARNED THAT A MAN HAD BEEN SHOT AND KILLED IN THE GUNFIGHT.

Clearly, my situation was very different. But the fact that I had been out so late during the middle of the season had still made headlines.

Coach Coughlin didn't scream or yell when I met with him in his office. He didn't fine or suspend me either. His first questions were about my family and my friends. He wanted to know if everyone was okay. I'm sure he was disappointed with me, but he didn't lecture me or lose his voice.

"You're a grown man, Victor," he said, after shutting the office door behind him. "I'm not going to tell you what you can or cannot do in your free time, but as someone who genuinely cares about you as a man, I can't understand why you'd be out at three in the morning. You've got too much ahead of you, son. Use this experience and move on."

We shook hands, and I thanked him. Coach Coughlin can be tough, and he gets on you for mental mistakes on the football field. But when it came to real life—the things that really mattered—there wasn't a more genuine and caring guy in the world.

OUR NEXT GAME was at home against the Eagles. They were without their starting quarterback, Michael Vick, and their top receiver, Jeremy Maclin, for our Sunday night showdown.

For whatever reason, we couldn't get anything going for three quarters. As we took the field in the fourth, we trailed 10–3. On third and long from our own twenty-nine, Eli found Hakeem deep down the right sideline for a first down. Two plays later, Eli rolled left out of the pocket and looked for me going deep.

The pass was perfect. I caught it, and ran it in for a touchdown.

The Eagles answered with their own touchdown, giving them a 17–10 lead with less than three minutes to go.

"Do you guys have another one in you?" Coach Sullivan yelled to Hakeem, Mario, and me.

On third and three, Eli called my number out of the shotgun and hit me on a quick slant pattern across the middle.

As Asomugha squared up to tackle me, I shifted my hips inside, then popped my body to the outside. I left him in the dust and ran thirty more yards to the sideline.

But on the very next play, Eli scrambled to his right and got the ball poked out from behind. The Eagles recovered the fumble, converted a first down, and ran out the clock. Another game, another loss.

I'D NEVER BEEN in a building as loud as the Superdome for our Monday night game versus the Saints.

Neither team scored in the first quarter, but their offense caught fire in the second. We trailed by eighteen points at halftime. Going into the fourth quarter, we trailed 35–10.

Down more than three touchdowns, Eli faked a handoff to Brandon and looked deep down the field for me. Because my defender had bit hard on Eli's play fake, I had several steps on him. The ball was thrown perfectly. I made the catch and ran it in for a seventy-two-yard touchdown.

A few drives later, I scored another touchdown. Still, it was too little too late. We lost again, our third straight defeat. We were now 6-5 for the year, with the undefeated defending Super Bowl champions, the Green Bay Packers, coming up.

I PLAYED WELL against the Packers, catching several passes and making some key blocks. Our two teams exchanged touchdown scores over the course of three quarters, and with 3:29 left to go in the game, Eli led us on yet another fourth quarter scoring drive. After the touchdown, D. J. Ware converted a two-point conversion to tie the game at 35.

MetLife was the loudest it'd ever been, and we all rallied for our defense to make a stop.

But Aaron Rodgers was just too good. The Super Bowl MVP from a year earlier hit Greg Jennings for eighteen yards, setting up a Mason Crosby thirty-yard field goal for the win.

It was our fourth straight loss.

MY FIRST STEPS inside Cowboys Stadium in Dallas were memorable. Eli and I walked onto the turf hours before the game and went through our routes. I remember eyeing the two scoreboards hanging above us. They must have each been 160 feet long and 80 feet wide. Everything was so *big*.

As Eli and I practiced our patterns, I considered what was at stake. A win, and we were still in the driver's seat of the NFC East. A loss, and our Super Bowl dreams would essentially be over.

I also thought about my father.

He had raised me a Cowboys fan. When his firefighter buddies used to say, "Your son is going to make it to the pros someday, Mike," he'd always smile and ask if they thought I'd be wearing the Dallas Cowboys star on my helmet. My father would have enjoyed seeing me compete anywhere, but he would have absolutely *loved* watching me play in Dallas.

Early in the first quarter, JPP got behind the Cowboys' offensive line and sacked Tony Romo in the end zone. Safety. JPP was having an incredible season, and that play got us off to the right start.

But things went downhill from there. With just over five minutes left in the game, Tony Romo threw a fifty-yard touchdown pass to a wide-open Dez Bryant.

We were now down 34–22 on the road in a rowdy building, and we hadn't won a game in over a month.

Eli led us down the field. He hit me for eleven yards and then again for eight more. On a crucial third and one, I ran a deep square out, and Eli found me for a twenty-three-yard pickup. Two plays later, he connected with Hakeem for twenty-four yards. Then, on second and eight, the offensive line gave Eli enough time to rifle a pass to Jake Ballard. With a man hanging on his back, Jake reached over the goal line for a touchdown.

We'd cut the lead to five, but the Cowboys controlled the ball and the clock. On third and five, Miles Austin, the Cowboys' star receiver, got wide open down the right side of the field. But Romo's pass wasn't perfect. It bounced off the ground incomplete. Now the Cowboys had to punt.

There we were, two minutes left, down five points, with a hostile opposing crowd calling us every name in the book.

What could be better?

Eli drove us right down the field again. He hit Ballard for twenty yards, me for eight, and then Ballard for another eighteen. On first and goal from the one, Brandon ran the ball up the gut of the Cowboys' defense for the go-ahead score. D. J. Ware converted for two points, and we took a 37–34 lead with just 1:30 remaining.

But the Cowboys wouldn't give up. They marched down the field with a pair of pass completions, and then their rookie kicker, Dan Bailey, trotted onto the field.

The ball was snapped, and Bailey booted the ball right through the uprights. Tie game. We were going to overtime.

Only, whistles were blowing. Coach Coughlin apparently had signaled for a time-out seconds before the Cowboys snapped the ball.

There'd be a do-over.

Bailey trotted back out onto the field, and I crouched on the sideline, thinking to myself, Man, somebody please block this kick. We needed someone to break through and make a play.

JPP did just that. He burst through the line and got his

fingers on Bailey's kick. It fluttered in the air and hit the ground. Game over.

We went wild on the sideline, jumping all over each other and then rushing onto the field.

The party carried over to the locker room, where we hugged and cheered.

Coach Gilbride, grinning from ear to ear, approached me at my locker. "Did you see what they were doing to you on those last few drives?" he asked.

I'd realized I was having trouble getting open, but didn't know how the Cowboys were keeping me contained.

"They put a double vise on you, Victor," Coach Gilbride explained. His smile widened. "That's the ultimate sign of respect for a wide receiver, son. The *ultimate*."

A "double vise" meant that Rob Ryan, the Cowboys' defensive coordinator, had ordered two different players to cover me. That made it tough for me, but it meant another player on our team was completely open.

We all congregated in the middle of the locker room, and Coach Coughlin told us to take a knee.

"Way to reach down, deep inside, and come up with the final courage to pull this thing out," he said as we clasped hands. Coach Coughlin then raised his right hand, and said, "What a tremendous job *in the division*. Let's enjoy this now, and I will see you . . . Wednesday!"

We all screamed in delight with that one.

■ ■ ■ ■

HOWEVER, WHEN WE took to the field the following Sunday against the 4-9 Redskins, we came out completely flat. The whole day had an incredibly weird feel to it. Sometimes you can just sense it in the air. The Redskins jumped out to an early 17–0 lead and we never came close to catching up. As we continued to make errors, the home crowd started to grumble.

But we just didn't have it.

We lost 23–10 and were back where we'd been the previous week—in a must-win situation.

THE JETS WERE 8-6, we were 7-7, and our seasons were both on the line. Throughout the week, it was the biggest sports story in New York.

Our team was fired up, the Jets were fired up, and both of our fan bases were ready to explode in the hours leading up to the game.

Both teams looked sluggish at the start. We had a horrible twelve-men-on-the-field penalty, and the Jets missed a makeable field goal. Our defense kept us in the game, though, and we trailed by just four points late in the second quarter.

Third and ten.

And the ball was on our own one yard line.

So much was going through my mind before the snap. Elaina was in the stands, eight months pregnant and ready to burst. Cromartie had nailed me with a big hit. Now Kyle Wilson was giving me some room on the line.

I caught Eli's pass, broke free of Wilson and Cromartie, and ran my fastest down the sideline, surging past the Jets' safety, Eric Smith.

I raced past the goal line, threw down the ball, and did the salsa in front of eighty thousand screaming fans.

The play not only gave us the game momentum, it flipped a switch on our season. The touchdown sucked the life out of the Jets' "home" crowd and gave our defense the breathing room it needed to stay aggressive.

We never looked back.

We beat the Jets 29–14, extending our season one more game and essentially ending theirs.

After the game, Peter John-Baptiste, one of the Giants' public relations guys, told me that there'd only been twelve ninety-nine-yard touchdown receptions in NFL history prior to mine. None had been by a New York Giant.

The play also made me the new Giants' single-season record holder for receiving yards in a season, breaking Amani Toomer's long-standing record of 1,343 yards.

WE PICKED UP right where we left off the following week. Our Sunday night week seventeen showdown with the Cowboys was hyped as "the Game of the Year" and the NFC East title hung in the balance.

In the first quarter, with the score still tied at zero, Eli hit me on the left side of the field. When I hauled the ball in, I was already past Terence Newman, the Cowboys' cornerback. I looked ahead and saw green grass. I ran hard, knowing both Newman and his teammate Gerald Sensabaugh were a step or two behind me. Instead of losing a second by turning around, I looked up at the scoreboard, using the video screen as my rearview mirror. I was able to separate from both of them and took the ball seventy-four yards for another score.

I did the salsa in the rain and was greeted with hugs by everyone on the sideline.

We were up 7–0 and didn't look back.

We won the game 31–14, celebrating our division title in the locker room. We were playoff-bound and would host the first-ever postseason game played in MetLife Stadium in exactly seven days.

My teammate Chris Canty, a former star on the Cowboys, approached me in the locker room after the win. "We're not division champions if you don't step up this season, Cruz," he said, patting me on the shoulder.

Chris Canty had been in the league seven full seasons and hadn't played in a Super Bowl. I thanked him for the compliment. I then assured him that we weren't done yet.

NEW
RESPONSIBILITIES

O N JANUARY 8, we hosted the Atlanta Falcons at MetLife Stadium. Elaina was in the stands, now nine months pregnant, with my mother seated beside her.

Eli had never won a playoff game at home, and many of the ex-players and analysts on TV picked us to lose.

Our defense stopped the Falcons on two big fourth-and-one plays, our running game took charge, and we had a 17–2 lead heading into the fourth quarter.

I'd been having trouble getting open all game, and though Hakeem and Mario were more than picking up the slack, I was growing frustrated with my performance.

"You see what they're doing to you, right?" Coach Ryan asked me after an offensive series in the second half. "They've got the double vise on you."

Well, that explained it. Hakeem caught six balls for 115 yards and scored two touchdowns. Mario had four receptions for sixty-eight yards and put the game away with a twenty-seven-yard touchdown reception in the fourth quarter. I caught just two balls for twenty-eight yards.

I couldn't have been happier.

We won 24–2, and Eli was finally able to celebrate a playoff victory in front of the home crowd.

WHEN ELAINA AND I got back to our apartment, I started to prepare some dinner. The Broncos-Steelers AFC wild card game was on TV, and Elaina was in the bedroom getting changed into something more comfortable.

"Victor!" she screamed.

"What is it, babe?" I answered, running over to see if she was okay.

"I think my water just broke."

The next few hours are a complete blur. I don't remember much, but I do know that I packed clothes in a gym bag. Lots and lots of clothes. I packed three changes of clothes for Elaina, two changes of clothes for Elaina's mother, some shirts for Malik if he decided to stop by, and some clothes for my mom and my little sister, Andrea.

What I forgot to pack was a change of clothes for *me*. No underwear. No socks. No second T-shirt. Nothing. I'd wear the same shirt, jeans, and underwear for the next eighteen hours.

I placed Elaina in the backseat of the car and rushed to Hackensack Hospital. When we got there, the nurses took Elaina into a room, and I immediately called my mother.

"What's up, Victor? Are you watching this game?"

"No, no. Mom—Elaina's giving birth!"

"What? Now?" she asked.

"Well, soon. But yeah!"

At ten twenty-four a.m. on January 9, 2012, Kennedy Ryan Cruz entered the world. She weighed seven pounds, two ounces and had beautiful, piercing gray eyes that lit up the room.

"You've got a beautiful mother, Kennedy. You know that?" I said, rocking her in the hospital room while smiling at Elaina.

I was the father of a wonderful, healthy baby girl.

I was truly blessed.

IT WAS DIFFICULT to focus on football that week. Every minute of every day, Elaina and Kennedy were on my mind. But when I got within the walls of our facilities, I shifted my attention to something else—the defending champion Green Bay Packers.

The Packers had finished the regular season with a 15-1 record and were a perfect 8-0 at Lambeau Field. Aaron Rodgers, the quarterback who had torn our hearts out with a last-second scoring drive back in December, had enjoyed an all-time great NFL season.

But we believed there was a chance Rodgers could be rusty. He hadn't thrown a pass in a game in twenty-one days. He also hadn't been sacked in twenty-one days.

Rodgers's coaches had sat him in week seventeen against the Lions, and the Packers had earned a bye during the first week of the playoffs. If our pass rush could get to him early, maybe he'd be off his game.

The Packers were nine-point favorites, but we'd won four straight games and felt very good about our chances.

As we hoped they would, our defensive line got to Rodgers early and often, pressuring him from all angles.

On third and eleven from deep in our own territory, the offensive line gave Eli time, and he threw a bullet pass to Hakeem across the middle. First down. On the very next play, Eli went back to Hakeem. This time, he not only caught the ball, but he bounced off a Packers defensive back and broke free in the open field. Sixty-eight yards later, he was beating his chest like a caveman in the end zone. We were up 10–0 on the defending Super Bowl champions.

Green Bay answered, though, and Rodgers led his offense right down the field for a touchdown. They blocked a field goal attempt on our next drive and had the ball again, looking to score once more.

"They're rusty," Justin Tuck shouted as our defense came off the field after James Starks, the Packers' running back, dropped an easy one in the flat. "They haven't played a big game in months."

Back and forth we went in the second quarter. We recovered a fumble in Packers territory with less than four minutes remaining in the half, but we couldn't punch the ball in for a touchdown. We settled for a field goal, giving us a 13-10 lead late in the second quarter.

We got the ball back, but deep in our own territory and with just forty seconds on the clock.

I expected Coach Gilbride to instruct Eli to kneel the ball a few times, preserving the three-point halftime lead. He had just the opposite in mind. "Let's go score some points," Coach Gilbride blared as our offense jogged back onto the field.

Eli hit Bradshaw for a few yards. Then he threw an incomplete to Jake Ballard.

It was third and one. You could feel the momentum swinging back and forth on every play.

During the time-out, Coach Gilbride drew up a running play for Ahmad.

"If you pop it to the outside, be sure to get out of bounds," he shouted. We had no time-outs left and though everyone *wanted* Ahmad to pick up a big gain, getting out of bounds and stopping the clock would give us two plays to set up for a field goal attempt before the end of the half.

Eli pitched it to Ahmad, and he picked up the first down, running behind David Diehl on the left side.

"Get out of bounds! Get out of bounds!" I shouted.

But Ahmad wasn't ready to just do that. Instead, he cut back and ran across the entire width of the field, picked up fifteen more yards, and somehow got out of bounds on the *right* sideline.

It was a risky but downright incredible play. The clock stopped, and we were now at the Packers' thirty-seven yard line with eight seconds left. Only enough time for one more play. The ball was out of Lawrence Tynes's field goal range, meaning Eli's only option would be to heave a prayer toward the end zone.

I'd never seen a team complete a Hail Mary pass in person. Not in high school, not in college, and certainly not in the pros.

The play is literally called "Trips, Hail Mary." It's in Coach Gilbride's playbook, and the instructions are as follows: "Run to the goalposts as fast as you can and try to catch the ball when it's thrown."

Usually on a Hail Mary pass, there are eight or nine defenders, but for whatever reason, we actually outnumbered them on that play. When Eli threw his pass high into the sky, Hakeem boxed his defender out like a basketball player positioning himself for a rebound. As the ball came down, he jumped as high as he could. The ball landed perfectly in his hands.

A Hail Mary!

The play sucked the life out of the entire stadium.

The defense carried us in the third quarter, sacking Rodgers play after play and keeping their high-scoring aerial game under wraps.

Lawrence Tynes hit a field goal to make it 23–13 to start the fourth quarter. We pleaded with our defense to stop the Packers again.

Rodgers tossed a screen pass to his running back, Ryan Grant, and Grant made a few nifty moves looking for extra yards. As he fought for a few more, Kenny Phillips, our strong safety, knocked the ball loose. Chase Blackburn scooped it up off the ground and ran forty yards the other way. He was brought down at the five yard line.

"Put 'em away!" Justin Tuck screamed as our offense took the field.

On the very next play, Eli faked a handoff to Ahmad and threw a perfect pass to a streaking Mario in the back of the end zone. Touchdown.

But the Packers wouldn't go away. They answered again with another touchdown, making the score 30–20.

"Hands team, get in there," shouted Coach Quinn. Green Bay was lining up for an onside kick. As one of the guys on "the hands team," I had to line up at the very front of our kickoff return formation. If you got your mitts on the ball, you needed to do everything—and anything—to ensure that you did not let it go.

Mason Crosby, the Packers' kicker, faked to his right and

booted the ball to the left in my direction. As it bounced off the ground, I kept my eyes on its laces, knowing it could take a funky twist or turn after ricocheting off the grass. The ball took a hop, I got both of my hands on it, and I fell to the ground, gripping it tightly to my chest.

The bottom of a pile-on is never fun. In that particular one, there were guys clutching my face mask, pulling my jersey, and grabbing my crotch.

I just closed my eyes and held on to the ball as tightly as I could.

The official signaled that we'd recovered the kick, and the pile of players was slowly ripped off me one by one.

The defense came up big on our next few drives, and after Brandon Jacobs scored a touchdown late in the fourth quarter, it became real—we were knocking the defending champs out of the playoffs and advancing to the NFC Championship Game.

CARLOS ROGERS.

It was the only name I heard about in the six days leading up to the NFC Championship Game against the 49ers.

Carlos Rogers.

All week, the beat reporters asked me if I'd be looking for revenge after he had mimicked my salsa dance two months earlier. I told the media that it hadn't really bothered me. The truth was, I'd been hoping to get another shot at him since the second we boarded the plane back to New York.

Salsa dance stuff aside, I didn't like that he'd outplayed me. I had a score to settle with Carlos Rogers.

We had watched tape of the loss in San Francisco and picked up some things. We saw that their safeties—Donte Whitner and Dashon Goldson—tried to get in and make a hit on every running play.

Seeing this on tape, our crew of receivers knew that we'd have to do more than just catch balls in the rematch. We'd have to really lend a hand in the blocking game too. Our efforts to protect Eli and our running backs would be as important as our catching passes.

It was all part of a cycle. If I blocked well for our running backs, they'd have a better chance at success. If they were having success, it'd force the San Francisco defense to respect our ground game. If the defense was concerned with our ground game, it would mean more opportunities for me through the air.

RIGHT FROM THE start, we tried establishing the run. I threw my body hard into Whitner and Goldson. It felt good getting a few solid hits on those guys. As strange as it sounds, it also felt pretty good getting hit *by* them. The rain was coming down hard, and my jersey was covered in mud.

As our running game got going, I found myself isolated one-on-one with Carlos Rogers. He wasn't talking trash, but he was grabbing me at the line. Eli spread the ball out over the first few drives, hitting Hakeem, Mario, and me early in the first quarter. But after the 49ers scored on a long pass play to make it 7–0, Eli told me he'd be coming to me more in the second quarter.

On a big third and six, he hit me for a thirty-six-yard completion. On the following third and four, we connected for six yards. First down. Four plays later, Eli tossed a beautiful pass to Bear Pascoe, our backup tight end, for a touchdown.

Over on our sideline, Eli pulled Hakeem, Mario, and me close to him. "You guys are open. They're blitzing me from all over, and they're honoring the run. You're all one-on-one with these corners. I'll find you."

He hit me for fifteen yards on our next drive, but we didn't put up any points. After both teams exchanged some punts, our offense took the field with less than two minutes remaining in the first half.

On second and ten, Eli found me for fifteen yards. I caught the ball, fought Rogers off, and picked up an additional four. Two plays later, he hit me for eleven more. On the very next play, Eli threw one deep to me. I had a step on Rogers, but the ball fell just beyond my grasp.

Back in the huddle, I told him, "It's there."

The very next play Eli threw me a seventeen-yard pass out of the shotgun, and I hauled it in to my body. Rogers, still covering me with no additional help, brought me to the ground.

In the huddle, Eli looked at me again. I knew he was coming right back to me.

Eli took the snap, and I made a hard cut over the middle. I had a step on Rogers, and Eli threw me a laser. I caught it with both hands, going down at the 49ers' twenty-one yard line.

I couldn't breathe. I was exhausted.

We hustled to the line, and Eli stopped the clock with a spike.

Lawrence Tynes then ran onto the field and booted one through the uprights for three points.

We had a 10–7 lead going into halftime.

Midway through the third quarter, the 49ers scored on a Vernon Davis touchdown, and we found ourselves trailing 14–10. Our offense stalled on our next few drives, and Eli took a beating behind the line of scrimmage.

But he got up whenever he was knocked down. The guy never seemed to flinch.

At the start of the fourth quarter, we were still behind 14–10. We had the ball on our own twenty yard line with a little over eleven minutes remaining.

But after three failed plays, it was fourth and fifteen

and our punt team was shuffling onto the field.

Steve Weatherford, our punter, booted one down the field, and Kyle Williams, the 49ers' punt return man, watched as it bounced off the ground and rolled past him. As the ball dribbled by Williams, Devin Thomas, our special teams "gunner," picked up the ball.

It didn't appear as though the ball had touched Williams at all, but Devin was insisting it had.

The officials ruled that the ball hadn't made contact with Williams. That made it the 49ers' football.

But Devin wasn't done. From the field, he urged the coaches to toss a red flag, challenging the ruling on the play. Coach Coughlin went for it, and the play was reviewed.

It turned out that Devin was right. The ball *had* hit Williams. On the replay, you could see the ball just slightly nick his knee. How Devin had noticed that, I'll never know. But it was the game-changing play we so desperately needed. Ed Hochuli, the official, came back on the field and awarded us the ball.

Then, on third and fifteen, from the 49ers' seventeen yard line, Eli took the snap out of the shotgun and waited for us to break out of our routes. I was open six yards over the middle, but he was going for it all.

He wound up and threw a perfect pass in the middle of the end zone, right where Mario was crossing at that exact moment. He jumped, and hauled it in for a touch-down.

But we hadn't won yet. On the 49ers' next possession, they tied it up at 17 with a field goal.

Over the next few drives, I was dinged up pretty bad. I was doing everything I could to get open, but I was taking a beating. On one play, I slipped on a route and my left foot came right out of its shoe. I walked back to the huddle with a soaking-wet foot, and my jersey covered in grass stains.

It was the toughest, most physical game I'd ever been in. After eight more minutes of our two teams exchanging punts, the game headed to overtime.

We won the coin toss and got the ball first, but we were stopped on our first drive. Then our defense came out and forced the 49ers to punt after three plays.

Our next drive started on our own thirty-five yard line. Eli hit my roommate Travis Beckum for five yards and then our fullback, Henry Hynoski, for three more. But just as we were moving the ball, Eli was sacked for a ten-yard loss.

Our punt team hustled back onto the field.

Devin Thomas had already made one game-changing play in the fourth quarter. Now we needed another one.

Weatherford's punt was a rocket in the air, and Kyle Williams caught it cleanly.

As Kyle Williams took a few strides with the ball, Jacquian Williams sprinted forty yards with a full head of steam. He let up for just a second, stretched his right arm out, and knocked the ball loose.

"Fumble!" I screamed, watching from the sidelines with Mario.

Devin Thomas jumped on the ball.

Four plays later, Lawrence Tynes kicked a thirty-one-yard field goal.

As the ball sailed through, I ran onto the field with my helmet in my hand, just screaming, "We're going to the Super Bowl! We're going to the Super Bowl!"

It was amazing.

MY BODY WAS a mess after the San Francisco game. I enjoyed having an entire week off with my baby girl before we headed to Indianapolis. Sometimes when I was holding her, she'd stretch her arms out. "Touchdown!" I'd say. Kennedy would smile back at me.

She was a natural.

On the Saturday before we left for the Super Bowl, the town of Paterson threw me an old-fashioned pep rally. I'd gotten word of it earlier in the week. I thought it was nice that a few of my friends and family members would see me off.

Not exactly. When I got to School 21, where the rally

was being held, *thousands* of Paterson residents were waiting for me.

I couldn't believe my eyes.

The word VICTOR-Y was spelled out in the windows of the school, and there were handmade signs that read CRUZ CONTROL. Congressman Bill Pascrell, the congressional representative from our district, was dressed in a blue Victor Cruz Giants jersey. The Eastside High School marching band was there in full force. The school's cheerleaders were doing Victor Cruz cheers. All of my old teachers, coaches, and friends from childhood flooded the streets. I saw several of my father's old firefighter buddies in the crowd, smiling proudly at me. Even Sister Gloria, my old principal from Paterson Catholic, made it to the rally.

I was introduced over a loudspeaker, and the entire crowd erupted with cheers.

I tend to have an answer for everything. But when I grabbed that microphone, I was speechless. I was overcome with raw emotion, just bowled over by the outpouring of warmth and love. When I finally got myself together, I thanked Coach Wimberly, Jim Salmon, and all the positive role models who had helped make me

BUT WHEN I GRABBED THAT MICROPHONE, I WAS SPEECHLESS.

the player—and more importantly, the man—that I had become. I thanked the teachers who helped me along the way, too.

I also thanked Paterson.

As I walked through the mob of kids, parents, and old familiar faces from the neighborhood, I linked eyes with an older woman a few hundred feet away. I recognized her immediately, and I felt my chest tighten seeing the tears flowing from her eyes.

I pushed through the jubilant crowd and wrapped my arms around her.

"This is for him," I wept. "I'm living out his dream. I'm living out *our* dreams."

The woman was Jordan Cleaves's mother.

I held Ms. Cleaves-Thompson in my arms, assuring her that I wasn't achieving my goals and chasing my dreams alone. Jordan was with me on the journey, and this outpouring of love and support wasn't just for me.

It was for both of us.

"He would have been so happy for you, Victor," she said. "He would have been so proud."

Two days later, we boarded the plane for Indianapolis.

FINISHING THE JOB

THE TUESDAY MORNING before Super Bowl Sunday is known as "Media Day." I'd heard all about it, but I still wasn't prepared for the sheer number of people that were on hand to ask us questions.

Some of those questions were about football.

The rest? Not so much. There were guys dressed as superheroes from Nickelodeon, supermodels asking questions about Tom Brady's UGG shoes, and comedians doing bits.

I got a kick out of getting the opportunity to answer some questions in Spanish. ESPN Deportes, Univision, and Telemundo all had camera crews in attendance. At one point, one of the stations took out a boom box and a disco ball and asked me to do the salsa. I was happy to oblige.

I loved connecting with the Spanish-speaking reporters. Though there had been others before me, I hadn't really had a Hispanic football or basketball player to look up to as a kid. If I could be that guy now for a young boy or girl, I'd be honored.

Super Bowl week, as a whole, made for a series of

surreal moments. On Monday night, a few of us went to dinner at a restaurant called St. Elmo's. Hundreds of fans lined up outside, just waiting for a glimpse of us. Everywhere we went over the next few days, there were Giants jerseys lining the streets. A lot of them were my number 80. Seeing the Giants' fans, out in full force, meant a lot.

As crazy as things were, I was happy both Elaina and Kennedy were with me the whole time. There was no way I could have spent an entire week away from them.

In addition to my mother, Elaina, and Kennedy, I secured Super Bowl tickets for Coach Wimberly, Jim Salmon, my brother, Malik, and my sisters, Andrea and Ebony. My *abuela* called me on the Friday before the game to tell me she'd be watching at home.

"And if you score," she said in Spanish, "don't forget to do your dance."

The coaching staff had prepared a game plan that we worked on at practice throughout the week. During walk-throughs, we were focused and energized. There were no distractions, no major hiccups, and nothing standing in our way.

I'VE ALWAYS TALKED to myself before games. I did it in high school, I did it at UMass, and I do it every week in the NFL.

At one point, as I was stretching, I repeated the same refrain over and over again: "It's about this team, man. It's about this team, man. It's about this team, man."

As a high school player, I'd fume when the college coaches talked to Chenry and Kit, jealous and confused because they weren't interested in me. In college, I'd call Liam from Paterson and ask him how all the other receivers were performing, but never thought to ask about how the team looked as a whole. Even in my rookie year, I sat and pitied myself because of my injury, but didn't feel the same kind of pain when the rest of the guys lost up in Green Bay.

Now, though, the *only* thing that mattered on the football field was whether we won or lost. I looked around and saw guys I loved and respected. I wanted to play my hardest and be spectacular so that *they* could be winners.

It was about the team.

It was about the New York Giants.

THE MOMENT I stepped onto the field, all the nervous energy, anxiety, and impatience of Super Bowl week disappeared. We were just playing football, like the kids on the street in front of my mother's house on East Eighteenth.

We got the ball first. On the third play of the game,

we were faced with a third and six from our own twenty-seven yard line. I'd been Eli's third-down go-to guy all season, and the Super Bowl would be no different. I made a move on my man and got open. Eli hit me with a pass, I picked up an extra yard, and we were on the move. First down.

I heard a recognizable roar in the crowd. "Cruuuuuuuz!"

Eli took us a bit farther down the field, but on third and thirteen, he was sacked for a loss. We punted the ball away and shifted our attention to the defense.

On the Patriots' very first offensive play, deep in their own territory, Tom Brady faked a handoff and looked for an open receiver. Everyone was covered. As Brady continued to search for an open man, Justin broke through the offensive line and dove at his legs. Brady, under pressure in his end zone, heaved the ball as far as he could to nobody in particular.

Flag on the play. Intentional grounding. And because Brady was standing in his own end zone, it was a safety as well.

That gave us a 2–0 lead and the ball back. It was early, but we had the momentum.

Our offense took the field, and Eli led us on another long drive.

He hit Henry Hynoski for thirteen yards. D. J. Ware popped open for eight more. Ahmad tore off a twenty-four-yard run. Eli then connected with Bear Pascoe and Hakeem for consecutive completions.

On third and three, Eli gave me the look. I knew the ball was coming my way. He hurried to the line and threw a short pass over the middle. I caught it with two hands and tried fighting for some more yards. As I pushed forward, though, Patrick Chung, a safety on the Patriots, jarred the ball loose.

Fumble.

The Patriots recovered.

I thought I might have been down before the ball got ripped from me, but I wasn't. The O line had been working so hard to give Eli enough time to pass, and I'd just let them all down.

I started to walk toward the sideline when I saw a yellow flag had been thrown.

It was a penalty against the Patriots. It turned out that New England had put twelve men on the field during the play instead of eleven. The penalty not only meant that we got the ball back, but we got a first down too.

I'd been given a second chance.

Two plays later, I got to the line of scrimmage and looked at the man standing five feet in front of me in a blue Patriots jersey.

It was James Ihedigbo.

Back in the fall of 2003, I had fallen in love with UMass

because of the two guys who took me around on my campus tour. Shannon James was one. The other was James Ihedigbo.

Staring at James, I thought of what Michael Strahan had told me that day in the mall. "The NFL will find you if you're good enough."

Now we were lined up, face-to-face, in the Super Bowl.

Eli took the snap and I ran directly at James. When he lunged to make contact, I made a quick slant to the inside and lifted my head. As I got a step on him, I saw the ball coming at me with one eye and a Patriots linebacker flying toward me with the other. Eli slipped the pass in between both James and the linebacker. The ball hit my chest. I bobbled it slightly, and then clutched it with both hands. I wasn't dropping this one.

I BOBBLED IT SLIGHTLY, AND THEN CLUTCHED IT WITH BOTH HANDS. I WASN'T DROPPING THIS ONE.

I got my feet planted, bounced off Hakeem, and heard the roar of thousands of Giants fans.

Touchdown.

I'd scored a touchdown in the Super Bowl, but what it meant for me personally didn't really register at the time.

We were up 9–0.

That was all that mattered.

■ ■ ■ ■

THE PATRIOTS ANSWERED. We knew they would.

Brady took New England the length of the field. But on third down, JPP batted down a pass, forcing the Patriots to settle for a field goal.

With a little over four minutes remaining in the second quarter, Brady got the ball back on New England's one yard line. With ninety-nine yards to go, he got hot. Pass after pass, Brady moved the Patriots down the field on a fourteen-play scoring drive. With just eight seconds to go he hit Danny Woodhead for a four-yard touchdown pass. The Patriots had a 10–9 lead as we headed into the locker room.

Halftime seemed to last forever. Usually, it's a quick fifteen-minute break before we head back onto the field. But because of Madonna's halftime show, we were in the locker room for close to thirty-five minutes.

When the third quarter finally started, the Patriots received the kick, and Brady went back to work. He led New England eighty yards, mostly out of the no huddle. A touchdown pass to Aaron Hernandez extended their lead. Though we'd started the game with an early lead, we were now trailing 17–9.

On our next offensive drive, it became clear—Hakeem and I weren't going to be the ones to beat the Patriots. Every time we lined up for a passing play, a cornerback would man up against us at the line, and then a safety would shade over after we broke into our routes.

Eli adjusted to the double coverage, throwing a series of passes to Jake, Bear, and Mario. Though we didn't score a touchdown on that drive, we picked up three points.

The Patriots now led by five.

Somehow, our defense needed to stop Brady. On third and eight, he went back to pass and looked for an open receiver. One second. Two seconds. Three seconds. After four seconds in the pocket, he took a step forward. Dave Tollefson, one of our defensive ends, hit Brady at the line and Justin tossed him to the ground. Quarterback sack.

On the next drive, Eli faked a handoff and threw a perfect pass to Hakeem. He took one step with the ball and had it stripped out of his hands.

Fumble.

Henry Hynoski had been running hard on the play, and he jumped on the loose ball.

Fumble recovered.

On third and eight, Eli looked for me, but I wasn't open. He was sacked, and we were forced to settle for another field goal. It was 17–15 Patriots.

"We need another stop, D!" I pleaded from the sideline.

New England had put up huge offensive numbers all season long and hadn't lost a game since we had beaten them on November 6. I knew if our defense could just stop the Patriots' offense one more time, we'd be able to find the end zone and win this game.

Chase Blackburn had once been the Giants' leading special teams tackler for six seasons. After the Giants had opted not to re-sign him over the summer of 2011, Chase waited for a shot with another team. For whatever reason, that shot never came. It looked like his NFL playing days were over. Still, he kept a packed suitcase with jeans, underwear, a few T-shirts, and a suit—just in case a team called and he needed to be somewhere on a moment's notice.

After a string of injuries decimated our linebacker corps in December, Chase's phone rang.

Two months later, Chase Blackburn was our starting middle linebacker in the Super Bowl.

On the second play of the fourth quarter, Brady took a snap out of the shotgun, avoided a sack, and rolled to his right. Evading the pressure of our surging defensive line, he looked deep for his six-foot-seven tight end, Rob Gronkowski. Brady wound up and threw a beautifully thrown ball deep down the field.

We all held our breaths on the sideline.

Chase isn't the fastest guy in the world, but he kept up with Gronkowski, running with him stride for stride. When the ball came down from the sky, Chase jumped up in front of Gronkowski and snatched it out of the air.

Interception.

"There we go, Chase!" I screamed, running onto the field with my helmet.

We were back in business.

DOWN 17–15 WITH fourteen minutes remaining, Eli started what we hoped would be another one of his classic fourth-quarter drives. But after a few completed passes—including an eight-yarder over the middle to me—we were stopped again and forced to punt.

The Patriots' next drive felt like it lasted even longer than halftime.

Brady was milking the clock as much as possible. On every third down, he'd make a play to move the chains and make it first and ten.

As minute after minute ticked off, I began to wonder if our offense would even get back onto the field. On second and eleven, Brady threw a deep pass to his top receiver, Wes Welker. There was a mix-up in our defense's pass coverage and Welker stood alone, wide open, at the twenty-yard line.

Brady and Welker had connected on 122 passes during the 2011 regular season. But when the pass left Brady's right hand, their timing was one second off. Welker jumped in the air, stretched both arms out, and went for the grab.

The ball flicked off his fingers and fell to the ground. Incomplete.

After another incomplete pass on third down, the Patriots punted with 3:46 left on the clock.

We'd get one last shot.

Coach Gilbride called in "Otter W Go" from the sideline. The play is designed for the two receivers lined up to the right of the line—Hakeem and me, in this case—to be the primary and secondary targets. Hakeem's supposed to go seven yards and cut inside. I'm supposed to do a double move and go deep.

The third option on the play, one that's not really expected to be used, is the receiver lined up on the left. That receiver, which in this case was Mario, is supposed to run a straight Go route down the sideline.

All game, Patrick Chung, the Patriots' safety, had been cheating off our other receivers to provide double coverage on Hakeem and me. Eli must have had a hunch that he'd be doing it again.

When he took the snap from the shotgun at our own seven yard line, Hakeem and I both ran our routes hard, fighting to get open. Eli looked at Hakeem, he looked at me, and then he shifted his hips to the left.

Without even taking a second to see what was downfield on the far sideline, he tossed a high, spiraling pass into the air.

Essentially, it was a no-look pass.

The pass went thirty yards in the sky and started to descend along the Patriots' sideline. Chung was a tenth of a second late getting to its landing spot. Sterling Moore, the cornerback covering Mario, trailed him by a step.

As the ball came down, Mario stretched out his arms as far as he could, simultaneously trying to keep both of his feet inbounds.

He caught the football, dragged his feet, and got pushed out of bounds by Chung. Mario went tumbling into a sea of Patriots players and coaches on their sideline.

But had he kept possession of the ball? Had both his feet stayed inbounds before he got hit?

The ruling on the field was a catch, but Bill Belichick didn't buy it. He immediately threw the red challenge flag.

Mario and I waited at midfield, watching the replay in slow motion on the stadium's video scoreboard.

It was a catch! It was as clear as day.

John Parry, the official, returned to the field and ruled it a reception. Thirty-eight yards. First down.

Only Eli and Mario weren't done.

Two plays later, they connected for sixteen yards. The play after that, they linked up for another two. Then Eli found Hakeem open along the sideline for fourteen. We were moving.

After another completion to Hakeem, we were well

within Tynes's field goal range. With a minute left to go, we trailed by two points.

On second and six from the Patriots' six yard line, Eli handed the ball off to Ahmad—and the Patriots gave him a free path to the end zone. I'd never seen anything like it. The entire defense just let him run the ball up the middle. There was no resistance.

It was a smart decision. If the defense had tackled Ahmad, Eli could have taken a few knees, killed the clock, and Lawrence Tynes would have kicked a game-winning field goal with no time left. But by letting Ahmad score a touchdown, Tom Brady and the New England offense would get the ball back, down four points with about a minute to go.

Ahmad got to the goal line, saw what was going on, and sort of awkwardly fell backward into the end zone for the touchdown.

It was the most anticlimactic last-minute touchdown score in Super Bowl history. None of us really cheered or congratulated him. We were too damn scared of Tom Brady.

It was 21–17. Our whole season was going to come down to one final defensive stand.

"We've done it all year, boys," I shouted to the D as they took the field.

Brady strolled out there like it was no big deal. Just

another Sunday. All the great quarterbacks act that way in high-pressure situations.

After two incomplete passes, Brady went back and looked deep for an open receiver on third down. Osi Umenyiora was pressuring him off the left edge, forcing him to shift to his right. Just as Brady took that step, Justin came surging up the middle and wrapped him up for the sack.

It was fourth and sixteen. The Lombardi Trophy was just one defensive stop away.

Unfortunately, it wasn't that easy.

Brady hit his receiver Deion Branch for nineteen yards and a first down.

I started pacing up and down the sideline again.

On the very next play, Brady connected with Hernandez for eleven more.

After a pair of incomplete passes, Brady broke from the huddle for the final play of Super Bowl XLVI.

The entire season would come down to a Hail Mary pass.

The last time we'd seen a Hail Mary thrown, Hakeem had come down with it in the end zone in Green Bay.

Brady took the snap out of the shotgun, danced a few steps behind the line of scrimmage, and evaded JPP's outstretched paw.

He cocked his arm back and heaved the ball fifty yards.

"Knock it down!" I screamed, hoping to will the ball to the ground.

The pass was thrown exactly where Brady intended— right in the middle of the end zone. The Lombardi Trophy was truly up for grabs.

Kenny leaped over Hernandez's back and swatted the ball with both hands.

Rob Gronkowski, Brady's other tight end, dove for it off the deflection, but he was too far away.

The ball hit the ground and trickled out of the end zone.

Incomplete.

Game over.

We'd just won Super Bowl XLVI.

As I ran onto the field looking for someone—anyone— to hug, I screamed like a little kid on Christmas.

I sprinted to Deon Grant and embraced him.

I found Chris Canty, the ex–Cowboys star who had come to the Giants three years before with dreams of winning a Super Bowl.

D. J. Ware. He'd been the guy who told me all about "Cut Day" and praying for the phone not to ring.

Michael Boley. Always the first one to greet me on the sideline after a touchdown.

I saw Chase Blackburn off in the distance. He'd made arguably the biggest play of the game and now would get his second Super Bowl ring.

Justin Tuck, Brandon Jacobs, Corey "CWeb" Webster, Antrel Rolle—I embraced them all.

Running around the field, just looking for more guys to hug, I thought about Rhett Bomar. What if Rhett hadn't thrown me the ball on just about every play of the final drive in that "meaningless" preseason game against the Ravens? Would I even have made the team? Rhett was probably with his family in a living room somewhere in Texas, but I knew he was watching the game. I knew he was rooting me on.

I thought about all of my old roommates. Tim Brown and Duke Calhoun with the Giants. Shawnn Gyles and Liam Coen up at UMass.

I thought about Jordan Cleaves.

As I bounced from one guy to the next, I saw Elaina and my mother running onto the field.

They weren't alone.

Malik, Ebony, and Andrea had somehow made it down there too.

"You know, Dad would have loved this," Malik said to Ebony and me. "He would have been jumping around, hugging more people than you, Vic. He would have been the loudest guy in the stadium right now."

Ebony laughed and kissed me on the cheek. "He would have been so proud of you, Victor."

Elaina and my mother were beaming. They'd both

been by my side for the whole entire ride. All the ups and all the downs.

They were two of the strongest, smartest, most beautiful women in the world. I looked at them and smiled, knowing my baby daughter had two wonderful women to watch and learn from.

Someone from the NFL called me up onto the podium, and I got to be one of the first players to hold the Lombardi Trophy. I grabbed it with both hands and just shook my head in amazement. Was it all really happening?

I looked over at Eli. He was cool and calm as always. He nodded at me and smiled. He was probably already thinking about off-season workouts in April.

Before we left the field, I made sure to take a few pieces of the confetti.

I'd been watching the Super Bowl since 1996, and the one thing I always remembered was the confetti after the games. I was bringing that Super Bowl confetti back home to Paterson no matter what.

LATER THAT EVENING, Elaina and I went back to our hotel room and kissed Kennedy good night. We got into bed and briefly talked about the game, the season, and how blessed we were to have met each other on that summer evening in 2004.

I shut the lights off and told Elaina I loved her.

Then I reached over to the nightstand and grabbed one of the pieces of confetti.

I held it tightly in my hands. I needed to feel that confetti just one more time.

It was real.

Everything was real.

I just wanted to make sure.

EPILOGUE

SIX WEEKS AFTER our team enjoyed a parade down New York City's Canyon of Heroes and received a glorious welcome from our fans back at MetLife Stadium, I was driving around Paterson and decided to drop by my old high school.

In 2010, Paterson Catholic had shut its doors, but the building had since reopened as a charter school called Paterson Charter School for Science and Technology. When I pulled into the parking lot, a wave of emotions washed over me.

I looked at "The Swamp," our old football field, and remembered all of those endless afternoons running my routes with Coach Wimberly screaming in the background. I thought of those glass cases in the hallways, filled with framed photographs of Tim Thomas and all of the Paterson Catholic greats before him. I remembered the rush of adrenaline I felt the first time I saw my face in one of the pictures. I thought of homeroom with Father Murphy, lunches in the cafeteria, and the thrill of walking into junior year biology class wearing my varsity jacket.

I got out of my car, walked through the building's front doors, and popped my head inside the school's main office unannounced.

Everything looked the same as it did eight years earlier, but *smaller*.

"Victor Cruz!" one of the women working in the main office shouted.

"Son, take a photograph with me! You must! You're my husband's favorite player on the Giants!"

I was happy to do so, but I started to worry that I was interrupting a school day.

The school principal came out from his office and introduced himself. But instead of asking me to leave, he urged me to take a walk around the school.

"These kids need to see you," he said. "They've got to see you in the flesh, walking these halls."

I wasn't quite sure what he meant, but I nodded politely and followed him out.

As we strolled through the building, more memories

came flooding back to me. I loved this school—regardless of what it was now called—and it felt good to be back.

Then the bell rang. End of period.

Within seconds, waves of students emerged from different classrooms and collided as one. They saw me, I saw them, and the reaction was sheer chaos. They slapped me five, they screamed, and they asked me for autographs. At one point, it got a little scary. There were thirty teenage kids—boys *and* girls—swarming me, just wanting to touch me. I looked at the principal, and he was smiling.

"This is nuts!" I shouted to him over the mob of hysterical students.

"Yeah, I had a feeling they'd get a kick out of this," he screamed back.

After a few minutes and several dozen autographs, we ducked back into the main office. I hadn't bobbed and weaved so hard since the NFC Championship Game. I was out of breath.

"Sorry if that was a bit overwhelming," he said, "but they needed to see you here. By seeing you in person, they know that your story is not some myth. They know that journeys like yours are, in fact, possible."

He then said something I'll never forget. "These kids

now know you didn't just come from out of the blue. They know that you came from within these walls and from these hallways. They know you came from Paterson."

He was right.

It may seem to football fans like I came completely out of the blue in 2011. Certainly my road was long, windy, full of hurdles, and even included some dead ends. I lost family. I lost friends. And on multiple occasions, I even lost my way.

When I reached what felt like rock bottom, I found a purpose to fight for my dreams. I realized I had a responsibility to the players that inspired me, the teammates who motivated me, everyone who believed in me, and to kids, like me, who just needed a chance.

The 2011 season was one I'll never forget, but it's just one piece of my life, a narrative that's only twenty-five years old and is still being written today.

What's most important in moving forward is not so much how I got here but what my journey has taught me:

You can't wait for your chance. You can't expect it. You have to earn it.

And, when you do, it's always with the help of others. So when you *do* get your shot, you carry on your shoulders the responsibility of validating the sacrifices everyone's made for you, the faith everyone has in you, and the trust you have in yourself to make the most of it.

This is my opportunity. And I'm playing to win.

NEW EPILOGUE

ONE YEAR REMOVED from the day we had left for the 2012 Super Bowl, I was lined up in the slot for a slant pattern pass from Eli. It was a play the two of us had run a thousand times, either in practice, the pre-season, or the fourth quarter of a tight game.

But this time the circumstances were different.

For all of the routes we had run together, Eli and I had never done it on a team of future Pro Football Hall of Famers.

Larry Fitzgerald, one of the greatest wide receivers ever, and a hero of mine when I was a fledgling player in college, was lined up next to me. Adrian Peterson, fresh off a regular season in which he had bounced back from knee surgery to rush for 2,097 yards, was in the backfield. Jason Witten, a Dallas Cowboys player I'd competed against my entire career, was shouting directions at me from his position on the offensive line.

We were all playing in the Pro Bowl, the NFL's annual All-Star Game. And while the stakes weren't nearly as high as they had been in the Super Bowl a year earlier, it was still pretty surreal.

I've been doubted my entire life, and even after my contributions to our 2011 Super Bowl season, plenty of skeptics remained. Over the summer I'd read some articles calling me a "One Hit Wonder." And after a rough game in week one versus the Dallas Cowboys in September, when I dropped three passes, the critics had come out in droves.

"Cruz didn't focus enough on football in the off-season."

"The success went to his head."

"He's not the player he was a season ago."

Yet, here I was, a few months later, playing in my first Pro Bowl. To get there, I had been voted in not only by the fans, but also by the NFL head coaches and my fellow players. I was one of just four wide receivers from a conference that includes Fitzgerald, Calvin Johnson, Dez Bryant, Julio Jones, Hakeem Nicks, Vincent Jackson, and Roddy White. It was really a tremendous honor.

Obviously, Eli and I would have rather been in New

Orleans preparing for another Super Bowl. But despite having the same nine wins we had gotten in 2011, defending the Lombardi Trophy wasn't in the cards for the 2012 New York Giants. We had been eliminated from playoff contention in week seventeen.

Though disappointed with the outcome, we had all agreed that we'd get back to work in April.

Meanwhile, Eli and I had one last slant pattern to run.

Wearing a Giants helmet and dressed in a blue-and-white jersey that read "National Football Conference," Eli took the snap. I broke into the old familiar route we'd been honing for the last three years. Five yards into the pattern, I shifted my hips and made my move on the cornerback covering me. I slid underneath his grasp, drifted into the end zone, and caught a perfect pass. Touchdown.

I looked up into the crowd, saw a bunch of fans smiling in anticipation, and I did the salsa.

At that moment, I knew that Abuela was smiling down on me from above.

She had passed away in September at the age of 77.

My grandmother had meant the world to me. Along with my mom, she was the most influential woman in my life. While sitting by her bedside during her final moments, I told her how much I loved her and how much of a role she had played in making me the man and father I am today. She smiled and held me close, like she'd done so many times before. She knew how much she meant to me. She was also very proud of the man I'd become.

Abuela was the one who had always kept me in line when I had gotten a bit out of control. When others had their doubts, Abuela was always certain that I'd make something out of my life. I will be forever grateful that she'd been able to enjoy some of the amazing events of the past few years. She had seen me make an NFL roster. She had seen me score touchdowns on Sunday afternoons. She had cheered me on as I performed the same dance I had once done in her kitchen.

Most importantly, she had met my beautiful daughter, Kennedy.

I understood that it was her time to go. I was at peace with it. I knew that God just wanted another angel up there with him.

A few days after her passing, we beat the Tampa Bay Buccaneers 41–34 at home in MetLife Stadium. Eli threw for 510 yards, including an eighty-yard touchdown pass to me. After scoring that touchdown, a pivotal one in the game, I did the salsa with a heavier heart than usual, knowing Abuela was not there to see it.

There were several other emotional moments during the 2012 NFL season. The most moving one, however, occurred off the field.

On the Friday before our week fifteen game against the Falcons, a lot was going through my head. Though we'd beaten the Falcons in the playoffs in 2011, they were 11-2 in 2012 and had yet to lose a game at home. Meanwhile, we needed a win to stay alive in the crowded NFC playoff hunt. In 2011 we had gone on an impressive late season run, but capturing that kind of magic two years in a row would be difficult.

In addition to football, Elaina and I were preparing for Kennedy's first Christmas. We wanted everything to be just right. The gifts, the decorations, the tree—there was a lot to do in a very short time. The holiday season had already arrived and we were way behind schedule.

All of those concerns were immediately put aside when I got home from practice that Friday afternoon. My mother had texted me to turn on the news. When I put on CNN, I saw that a terrible tragedy had occurred in Newtown, Connecticut. A gunman there had killed twenty children and six adult staff members at Sandy Hook Elementary School.

Elaina and I couldn't wrap our heads around the tragedy. The more we learned about it, the sadder we felt. The world can be so confusing sometimes.

I left for Atlanta early the next morning, but not before I had savored every last second with my family. When we got to our hotel, I turned on my iPhone to find hundreds of tweets directed at me.

Several of them had the same message.

Jack Pinto, one of the young victims in the shooting, had apparently been a big fan of mine. He had worn my jersey to school just about every day and often did the salsa dance in the classroom and in the halls.

My Twitter followers told me all about Jack. Though just a six-year-old boy, he had been a positive light in everyone's life and an inspiration to all who knew him.

I knew the Pintos were grieving and going through an unthinkably painful period, but I wanted to send my condolences. Elaina helped me find the Pintos' phone number. I asked her to join me on the call to the family. I needed her support.

We dialed the number. I'd never made a phone call like this in my life and waited nervously for it to go through.

"Hello?" It was Jack's father, Dean.

I introduced myself to Mr. Pinto. I told him how incredibly sorry I was for his loss. Dean thanked me for calling and told me that Jack's older brother Ben, an eleven-year-old, was a big fan of mine as well.

I respectfully asked if he could put Ben on the line.

I remember being eleven years old.

I remember not knowing much about the ways of the world, but looking up to my sports idols. I remember the Anfernee "Penny" Hardaway poster in my basement, the Michael Jordan sneakers on my feet, the Deion Sanders jersey I wore everywhere. If hearing my voice could give Ben Pinto a lift during his darkest of days, I wanted to give him that moment.

So we spoke. Ben was hanging in there. He was far stronger than I ever was at that age.

The next morning, I wrote the words "My Hero" and "R.I.P. Jack Pinto" on my cleats and gloves. We lost the game to the Falcons, but I was incredibly proud to play with Jack Pinto's name on my uniform.

On Monday, Elaina, Kennedy, and I drove from New Jersey to Newtown, Connecticut, to visit the Pinto family. Dean and his wife, Tricia, were wonderful. I gave my cleats and gloves to Ben, and we played a game of *Madden* in the family's living room. I picked the Giants as my team in the video game. So did he.

We had come to Newtown to mourn the death of a young boy.

We ended up celebrating his life, instead.

Jack Pinto was buried in a Victor Cruz jersey. You hear something like that and you don't know whether to say you appreciate it or just to let it be. It leaves you kind of blank. It leaves you speechless.

But I will be forever moved by it.

THAT FOLLOWING SUNDAY, we lost to the Ravens in Baltimore. Led by quarterback Joe Flacco, they had the look and feel of a team of destiny. To be honest, they reminded me a lot of how we had looked a year earlier.

Six weeks later, the Ravens were hoisting the Lombardi Trophy in the Superdome as Super Bowl XLVII champions. Just as we had done in 2012, Baltimore had won a home game in the wild card round of the playoffs before going on the road to win in the divisional and championship rounds. Then they had gone to New Orleans and beaten the San Francisco 49ers 34–31 in an exciting Super Bowl.

Though I would have much rather been playing in the game myself, I was happy to see my friends Ray Rice and James Ihedigbo get the opportunity to bask in that glory.

The 2012 NFL season was undoubtedly a memorable one. I grew as a football player, and I grew as a man. I believe I am a better player now than I was a year ago. I am a better father too.

Making the Pro Bowl was a personal goal of mine, and though we didn't make the playoffs, I'm confident we have the pieces in place to make another Super Bowl run next season.

Amazingly enough, Super Bowl XLVIII will be played at MetLife Stadium. As the first outdoor "cold weather" Super Bowl in NFL history, it may be windy, snowy, and minus ten degrees at the opening kickoff.

In other words—just the way we like it.

As I look ahead, I see a wide-open field. There's still so much more I want to accomplish, both on the football field and off. Kennedy's just starting to walk, and it's amazing to watch her grow up. She lights up when she sees my face and I'm told she giggles when she hears my voice on television. I'm never happier than when I'm relaxing on the living room couch with her and Elaina.

Everything's great, but you can never be satisfied.

I'm not satisfied.

Trust me, I'm just getting started.

ACKNOWLEDGMENTS
VICTOR CRUZ

At first, I thought all that went into writing a book would be overwhelming. I envisioned it being a slow and tedious process. I also feared that I wouldn't remember everything that's occurred in my life and that some key moments of my journey would go missing from the overall narrative. But as I started to talk with Peter about my childhood, it all started to come to me rather easily and we ended up having a lot of fun.

Writing this book turned out to be a great experience and I'd definitely do it all over again if I had to. If my life story can inspire one kid or change just one life, all the hours and all the hard work that went into this project would be more than worth it.

First, I want to thank Peter Schrager. He is, in my opinion, one of the best young writers today and we worked incredibly well together. Upon meeting him, I learned that not only did Peter already know most of my story, but he was genuinely enthused about being given the opportunity to share it with the world. I was confident that he'd do a great job and he did. We had a great time writing this book together.

I'd also like to thank Carlos Fleming and everyone at IMG for making this book a reality. Thanks to Scott Waxman for helping us in putting all the pieces together. Thank you, Ray Garcia, Mark Chait, and the rest of the Penguin/Celebra team, including Kara Welsh, Craig Burke, and Julia Fleischaker.

Finally, I'd like to thank the special people who've helped make all of my life's dreams come true.

Coach Wimberly, Jim Salmon, and the rest of my coaches and teachers growing up—thank you for your guidance and constant belief in me.

My mother, Blanca, you're the strongest woman I know. Everything I do, everything I achieve, is a reflection of you.

My sister Andrea, my sister Ebony, my brother, Malik— you've always been there and we've been through a lot. Our experiences together have shaped us into the people we are today. We've shared all of the highs and all of the lows, and you'll be with me for all that's still to come.

Abuela, you've dedicated your life to ensuring your

family is happy and their lives are fulfilled. You taught me the salsa, yes, but that's just a tiny part of the impact you've made on me.

Kennedy, you're my angel and my inspiration. You'll always be Daddy's Little Girl and my life's greatest accomplishment.

Elaina, I love you. I've been yours since the first night we locked eyes and you've been with me for every step along the way. This book would have never come to fruition without your and Brand Infinite's determination and vision. I'm not the man I am today without you by my side.

ACKNOWLEDGMENTS
PETER SCHRAGER

Vic, thank you for the opportunity of a lifetime. You're a tremendous person and I'm forever changed from having met and worked with you on this project. You said that you were in awe of the effect Michael Strahan had on those Giants fans at the mall back in 2007. You don't even realize how much you've impacted the lives of the individuals you've crossed paths with over the course of your twenty-five years. You're just getting started, my man, and I can't wait to see what's next for you. That next slice of bruschetta pizza (covered in crushed red pepper, of course) is on me. Keep on "peacocking," Mr. *GQ*. Keep on loving life.

Elaina, thank you for so graciously opening the doors to your lives to me. Kennedy, thank you for being so amazingly well behaved when Daddy was juggling "writing duty" with "baby duty."

Carlos Fleming, Scott Waxman, and Ray Garcia—thanks for taking a shot on a first-time author with big-time dreams. Mark Chait, you're an incredible editor and an even better hand-holder. Your late-night pep talks could rival Coach Coughlin's best locker room speeches. Kerri Kolen, thank you for being my own personal Chris Pettit. I never would have gotten this opportunity without your encouragement and faith. Eric Gillin, thanks for your eyes, your red marker, and our shared appreciation for early morning Dunkin' Donuts runs. Rick Jaffe, Jeff Husvar, Jed Pearson, Steve Miller, Nancy Gay, Alex Marvez, and Todd Behrendt at FoxSports.com—thank you for all the wonderful opportunities and experiences over the years. Devin Gordon and Sean Fennessey at *GQ*, Matt Sullivan at *Esquire*—the same goes to you guys. Dave, Abbie, Arleen, Bruce, and the rest of the Edelman gang—thanks for your unwavering support. John Bolster and Tom Seeley, we're long overdue for drinks. One of these years, I promise. Thanks to Steve Sobol, Jason Weber, and the rest of the NFL Films team for lending Vic and me the keys to your castle for a day.

Mom, Dad, and Justin—thanks for tolerating all those rides up to Grandma Rhoda's house, where I recited made-up stories I'd written about Drazen Petrovic, Derrick Coleman, Kenny Anderson, and the 1992 New Jersey Nets. Then, now, always—you've been champions.

Most important, thank you, Erica, for being my everything. I'm not sure how this—or anything—gets done without you cheering me on. I love you.